THE NEW LAW OF SEXUAL OFFENCES
IN SCOTLAND
SUPPLEMENT I TO VOLUME II OF
GORDON'S CRIMINAL LAW

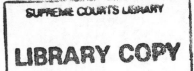

THE NEW LAW OF SEXUAL OFFENCES IN SCOTLAND:
SUPPLEMENT I TO VOLUME II OF GORDON'S CRIMINAL LAW

by

James Chalmers
Senior Lecturer in Law, University of Edinburgh

Published under the auspices of
THE SCOTTISH UNIVERSITIES INSTITUTE

W. GREEN   THOMSON REUTERS

Published in 2010 by Thomson Reuters (Legal) Limited
(Registered in England and Wales,
Company No 1679046.
Registered office and address for service
100 Avenue Road, Swiss Cottage,
London, NW3 3PF) trading as W. Green

Typeset by Matthew Marley, Devon
Printed and bound in Great Britain by CPI Antony Rowe, Chippenham
and Eastbourne

No natural forests were destroyed to make this product;
only farmed timber was used and re-planted.

A catalogue record for this title is available
from the British Library

ISBN 978-0-414-04127-1

PREFACE

A full account of the aims and scope of this book can be found in the "introduction and scheme", below. It is not intended as the last word on its subject matter, particularly as the relevant legislation was still not in force at the time of writing. While, when the English law of sexual offences was reformed by the Sexual Offences Act 2003, that statute was brought into force within six months of Royal Assent, the Scottish legislation seems to be too much of a shock to the system for such haste. The 2009 Act received Royal Assent on July 14, 2009. At the time of writing, there was still no publicly announced commencement date for the 2009 Act, although a consultation document published by the Scottish Government on draft national guidance regarding underage sexual activity in April 2010 stated that the Act was "due to commence later this year". The text proceeds on the basis that the Act has been brought into force in its entirety.

It has, as ever, been a pleasure to work with W. Green. I am particularly grateful to Philippa Blackham and Mark Reid for their careful editorial work, and also to all other staff at Greens who have been involved with the book, including Alan Bett, Janet Campbell and Jill Hyslop. In the preparation of the text, I have benefited from conversations with colleagues including, amongst others, Sharon Cowan, Alistair Devlin, Christopher Gane, Fiona Leverick, Gerry Maher and Findlay Stark, but none bears any responsibility for such errors or infelicities as the text may contain. It is an enormous privilege for this book to be published both in the Scottish Universities Law Institute series and as a supplement to Sir Gerald Gordon's *The Criminal Law of Scotland*. Like all those who write on Scots criminal law, the present author is immeasurably in Sir Gerald's debt.

James Chalmers
June 2010

CONTENTS

CHAPTER 2

THE SPECIAL PART

CHAPTER 3

THE PROSTITUTION (PUBLIC PLACES) (SCOTLAND) ACT 2007

TABLE OF CASES

TABLE OF STATUTES

Acts of the Scottish Parliament

TABLE OF STATUTORY INSTRUMENTS

TABLE OF SCOTTISH STATUTORY INSTRUMENTS

LIST OF ABBREVIATIONS
(excluding standard law reports and journals)

2009 Act

Sexual Offences (Scotland) Act 2009.

Alison, *Principles*

Alison, A., *Principles of the Criminal Law of Scotland* (Edinburgh: Blackwood, 1832).

Brown, *Sexual Offences (Scotland) Act 2009*

Brown, A.N., *Sexual Offences (Scotland) Act 2009* (Edinburgh: W. Green, 2009).

Burnett, *Criminal Law*

Burnett, J., *A Treatise on Various Branches of the Criminal Law of Scotland* (Edinburgh: Archibald Constable and Co, 1811).

Card, Gillespie and Hirst, *Sexual Offences*

Card, R., Gillespie, A.A., and Hirst, M., *Sexual Offences* (Bristol: Jordans, 2008).

Discussion Paper

Scottish Law Commission, *Discussion Paper on Rape and Other Sexual Offences* (The Stationery Office, 2006), Scot. Law Com. D.P. No.131.

Gordon, *Criminal Law*

Gordon, G.H., *The Criminal Law of Scotland*, edited by M.G.A. Christie, 3rd edn, 2 vols (Edinburgh: SULI/W. Green, 2000, 2001).

Hume

Hume, D., *Commentaries on the Law of Scotland, Respecting Crimes*, edited by B.R. Bell, 4th edn (Edinburgh: Bell & Bradfute, 1844).

Macdonald, *Criminal Law*

Macdonald, J.H.A., *A Practical Treatise on the Criminal Law of Scotland*, edited by J. Walker and D.J. Stevenson, 5th edn (Edinburgh: W. Green, 1948).

Policy Memorandum

Scottish Parliament, *Sexual Offences (Scotland) Bill: Policy Memorandum* (Scottish Parliament, 2008).

Report

Scottish Law Commission, *Report on Rape and Other Sexual Offences* (The Stationery Office, 2007), Scot. Law Com. No.209.

Rook and Ward, *Sexual Offences*

Rook, P., and Ward, R., *Rook and Ward on Sexual Offences: Law and Practice*, 3rd edn (London: Sweet & Maxwell, 2004).

INTRODUCTION AND SCHEME

This short book is intended as a supplement to the third edition of Gordon's *Criminal Law*[1] to take account of the effect of the Sexual Offences (Scotland) Act 2009.[2] The 2009 Act, which is the result of a review conducted by the Scottish Law Commission,[3] creates an entirely new law of sexual offences for Scotland, with some exceptions: the Commission's consideration of offences relating to "public morality" was limited and no recommendations were made for reform in certain specified areas, including incest.[4]

Because the 2009 Act rewrites the law of sexual offences comprehensively, this supplement does not adopt paragraph and chapter numbers corresponding to the third edition of Gordon's *Criminal Law*. It may therefore be consulted as a standalone text. In accordance with the drafting technique used in the 2009 Act, "A" is used to denote the individual accused of a sexual offence and "B" the complainer. For consistency, this has been done even where reference is made to the pre-2009 law.

The treatment of the 2009 Act in this book is divided into two chapters. Chapter 1 is the "general part", discussing provisions which are common to the scheme of the 2009 Act as a whole, such as consent, the definition of "sexual", and the requirement (where consent-based offences are concerned) of an absence of reasonable belief in consent, as well as procedural issues relating to resolution of temporal uncertainty and uncertainty as to age.

Chapter 2 is the "special part", discussing the specific offences created by the Act. Where an offence definition is comprised wholly or mainly of elements which are common to the Act as a whole, these are not discussed further. This means, for example, that the treatment of rape itself is relatively brief, because the key components of that offence—an absence of consent on B's part and the absence of any reasonable belief in consent on the part of A—are both discussed fully in Ch.1. Because the child offences created by Pt 4 of the Act mirror the general offences created by Pt 1, child offences are not discussed separately.[5] Instead the relevant offences are grouped together as appropriate. To assist the reader, a table has been included at the beginning of Ch.2 listing each offence created by the Act, the section of the Act which creates it, and the paragraph number identifying the text where that offence is discussed.

Although criticism is made of various aspects of the Act, this book is not a critical evaluation of the Act as a whole nor of the process which led to its

---

[1] Gordon, *Criminal Law*.

[2] It also includes a brief note on the provisions of the Prostitution (Public Places) (Scotland) Act 2007: see below, Ch.3.

[3] See *Report*; Pamela Ferguson, "Reforming Rape and Other Sexual Offences" (2008) 12 Edin. L.R. 302; S. Cowan, "All Change or Business as Usual? Reforming the Law of Rape in Scotland" in C. McGlynn and V.E. Munro (eds), *Rethinking Rape Law: International and Comparative Perspectives* (London: Routledge Cavendish, 2010), p.154.

[4] And also bestiality: see *Report*, paras 5.2–5.4. Prostitution, pornography and adult entertainment were considered by the Commission to be outwith the scope of its project: *Report*, paras 1.13–1.16. The Commission discussed necrophilia and recommended that consideration be given to the creation of an offence of unlawful interference with human remains, but took the view that as such an offence covered "more than sexual activity", it was beyond the scope of the review: *Report*, paras 5.28–5.29.

[5] A discussion of the general issue of the age of consent can be found in Ch.1 of this book: see below, paras 1.15–1.18.

enactment.[6] While it is impossible to produce an authoritative treatment of the Act's provisions before it has even come into force, it is hoped that the account provided is sufficiently detailed and thorough to amount to useful guidance on this new legislation. At the time of writing, no commencement date had been set for the Act, but the text proceeds on the assumption that it has been brought into force in its entirety.

---

[6]   For critical accounts of sexual offences reform in recent years, see Jennifer Temkin, *Rape and the Legal Process*, 2nd edn (Oxford: Oxford University Press, 2002); McGlynn and Munro, *Rethinking Rape Law*, 2010.

Chapter 1

THE GENERAL PART

What is "Sexual"?

Many offences under the 2009 Act require the prosecution to show that certain **1.01** conduct[1] was "sexual".[2] For example, the offence of sexual assault by penetration requires that A, "penetrates sexually to any extent" the vagina or anus of B[3]; sexual assault can be committed where A, "intentionally or recklessly touches B sexually"[4]; and sexual exposure requires that A's genitals are exposed, "in a sexual manner" to B.[5] Other offences require proof that an image of a sexual activity[6] or communication[7] is sexual, while voyeurism requires that A act for the purpose of "obtaining sexual gratification" (or, alternatively, "humiliating, distressing or alarming B").[8]

The 2009 Act goes no further in defining this core concept than to say (in s.60(2)) that[9]:

> "For the purposes of this Act—
> (a) penetration, touching, or any other activity,
> (b) a communication,
> (c) a manner of exposure, or
> (d) a relationship,
> is sexual if a reasonable person would, in all the circumstances of the case, consider it to be sexual."

This definition was intended by the Scottish Law Commission as an "objective test".[10] It seems to follow that any particular predilection or motive on the accused's part does not form part of the "circumstances of the case".[11] Therefore, for example, if an accused attempts to remove a shoe from a girl's foot

---

[1] Usually the accused's, but not always: see, e.g. 2009 Act ss.4 (sexual coercion) and 5 (coercing a person into being present during a sexual activity).

[2] Indeed, the only offences where it is *never* necessary to prove this specifically are rape, rape of a young child and having intercourse with an older child (2009 Act ss.1, 18, 28), penile penetration of the vagina, anus or mouth effectively being deemed to be sexual. Specific proof is also unnecessary where sexual assault is committed by the ejaculation of semen over B (2009 Act ss.3(2)(d), 20(2)(d)), where voyeurism is committed by observing non-sexual private acts for the purpose of humiliating, distressing or alarming B (2009 Act ss.9, 26, 36, all of which must be read together with s.10) and where an offence of coercing a person into or causing a child to look at a sexual image is based on an image of genitalia (2009 Act ss.6, 23, 33).

[3] 2009 Act s.2.

[4] 2009 Act s.3(2)(b). This is one of five "things" specified in s.3(2) which can amount to the offence.

[5] 2009 Act s.8.

[6] 2009 Act s.6 (coercing a person into looking at a sexual image). Although the definition of "sexual" in s.60(2) does not refer directly to images, the fact that it refers to "activity" is sufficient to make it applicable given that the image must be of a sexual activity.

[7] 2009 Act s.7 (communicating indecently, etc.).

[8] 2009 Act ss.9, 26, 36. The definition of "sexual" in respect of this offence may differ from the rest of the Act: see below, para 1.02.

[9] The definition of sexual is the same as that proposed by the Scottish Law Commission: see *Report*, paras 3.42–3.44.

[10] *Report*, para.3.43.

[11] cf. *R. v Court (Robert Christopher)* [1989] A.C. 28. But if the accused openly discloses this motive so that an observer would be aware of it, it presumably can be taken into account.

because it gives him sexual gratification, he is not guilty of sexual assault.[12] The Commission noted that the court would still have the power to invoke the sex offender notification procedure in such cases on the basis that there was, "a significant sexual aspect to the offender's behaviour in committing the offence",[13] without comment on the peculiarity that this would mean regarding the accused's behaviour as non-sexual for the purposes of establishing guilt but sexual for the purposes of disposing of the case thereafter.[14]

Under the s.60(2) definition, the sexual nature of physical conduct does not depend on direct contact with genitalia or breasts—although certain offences may require that because of other aspects of their definition. In the English case of *R. v H*,[15] where the defendant made a sexual proposition to the victim and then attempted to pull her towards him by grabbing at her clothing, it was held that this could properly be regarded as sexual in nature. Although the Scottish legislation is differently formulated, the same result should obtain.

Beyond the implicit lack of any requirement for direct physical contact, the drafting of s.60(2) gives no explanation of just what it means for something to be "sexual".[16] The term can be understood in a number of different ways, the most relevant of which are first, pertaining to the sexual organs and secondly, pertaining to the gratification of sexual appetites.[17] Assuming that both are relevant here, is a medical examination of genitalia "sexual", on the basis that it pertains to the sexual organs? One authoritative commentator on the equivalent English legislation, where the term is similarly undefined, suggests yes, albeit that such conduct will normally be justified by consent or necessity.[18] The explanatory notes to the English Act, however, reach a directly contrary conclusion.[19] A less ambiguous approach would be to say that something is sexual, "if carried out with a view to the gratification of [the actor's] sexual appetites",[20] but that would introduce an unwelcome element of purpose into the definition, and would mean that many assaults which would be regarded as obviously sexual would fall outwith the ambit of the 2009 Act if doubt could be raised as to whether the accused's purpose was to humiliate the victim rather than to obtain sexual gratification.

---

[12] The facts are those of *R. v George* [1956] Crim. L.R. 52; cf. *R. v Price (David Arthur)* [2003] EWCA Crim 2405; [2004] 1 Cr. App. R. 12.

[13] Sexual Offences Act 2003 Sch.3 para.60. See *Report*, para.3.43.

[14] While odd, this may be justified on the basis that the conduct does not violate the victim's sexual integrity (and is therefore not a sexual offence) but does indicate a propensity towards sexual offending (and the sex offender notification procedure should therefore apply).

[15] *R. v H (Karl Anthony)* [2005] EWCA Crim 732; [2005] 1 W.L.R. 2005.

[16] The Scottish Law Commission rejected the definitional provisions found in the English legislation (Sexual Offences Act 2003 s.78) as "too complex", noting that they had been criticised by J.R. Spencer, "The Sexual Offences Act 2003: (2) Child and Family Offences" [2004] Crim. L.R. 347, 348. But Spencer's criticism was that the English definition was, "rather delphic": the Scottish definition is equally so in that both leave the term "sexual" itself undefined. The Canadian courts experienced some difficulty with the term "sexual" in the past, holding that where A assaulted B by fondling her breasts, such an assault was inherently not sexual. The Supreme Court eventually resolved the matter in favour of the contrary position—see *R. v Chase* [1987] 2 S.C.R. 293—but without offering a clear definition of the term.

[17] The definition found in the *Oxford English Dictionary* is rather more detailed than this, and its relevance to the statutory use of "sexual" is discussed carefully by Francis Bennion, "The Meaning of 'Sexual' in the Sexual Offences Bill 2003" (2003) 167 J.P. 764.

[18] Andrew Ashworth, *Principles of Criminal Law*, 6th edn (Oxford: Oxford University Press, 2009), p.333. Even if the doctor secretly obtains sexual gratification from the examination, this would not render his actions a sexual assault provided that the examination was properly carried out for legitimate medical purposes: see *R. v Court (Robert Christopher)* [1989] A.C. 28, per Lord Goff of Chieveley at 49.

[19] Sexual Offences Act 2003 explanatory notes para.146.

[20] Bennion, "The Meaning of 'Sexual' in the Sexual Offences Bill 2003" (2003) 167 J.P. 764, 766.

An alternative approach would be to regard an act as sexual if a reasonable person would regard it as pertaining to the sexual organs or as being carried out for sexual gratification, although that may run the risk of being over-broad.[21] A kiss could be regarded as sexual where its nature and extent was such as to go beyond a demonstration of affection.[22] The example of the doctor is potentially a misleading one, given that there should be no need to rely on the construction of "sexual" to take such actions outwith the scope of the criminal law. An individual's sexual integrity may be violated by an assault even where the accused's purpose was not one of sexual gratification, and the labelling of such acts as sexual assaults properly reflects the wrong done to the victim.

Sexual gratification in voyeurism

The s.60(2) definition does not apply to the purpose of "obtaining sexual grati- **1.02** fication" which may form part of the case against the accused in a voyeurism prosecution. It is unclear whether this is deliberate: the Scottish Law Commission did not contemplate an offence of voyeurism, which was introduced into the Act by amendments at Stage 2.[23] Given that the purpose of "gratification" is personal to the accused in a manner differing from the items specified in s.60(2), there may be good reason for holding that "sexual gratification" can be established in such a case even if a reasonable person would not have been gratified in this way. The fact that voyeurism must be committed in relation to a "private act"[24] avoids the offence being thereby given excessive breadth.

CONSENT

At common law, the meaning of consent received little judicial attention.[25] In **1.03** *Marr v HM Advocate*,[26] where a jury asked the sheriff for guidance on consent, the appeal court endorsed the sheriff's response that the, "definition of consent is a common, straightforward definition of consent. It's the common English word given its normal meaning".[27] The only areas where the criminal law might have been regarded as giving any kind of special or technical meaning to sexual consent were where it was alleged that the consent had been negated by fraud as to identity or the nature of the act, and even there the rel-

---

[21] See, e.g. *R. v Leather (Nicola Jane)* (1993) 14 Cr. App. R. (S.) 736, where the defendant grabbed hold of the complainant's testicles and squeezed. Such an assault would not normally be regarded as sexual (assuming A's intention was merely to inflict pain on B), nor would it seem to justify invoking the sex offender notification procedure. But cf. the assault in *Re Attorney General's Reference (No.65 of 1999)* [2000] 1 Cr. App. R. (S.) 554, where the defendant engaged a prostitute and surreptitiously put live maggots into her vagina. That was treated as an indecent assault, but how does it differ in principle from the facts of *Leather*? It might be argued that the act is somehow related to sexual gratification in a way that the *Leather* assault was not, even if such gratification were not the defendant's motive, but this does not seem a particularly satisfactory test. Alternatively, the assumption that an assault such as that in *Leather* is not a sexual assault may simply be incorrect.

[22] cf. *Moynagh v Spiers*, 2003 S.L.T. 1377.

[23] See Brown, *Sexual Offences (Scotland) Act 2009*, p.33. The explanatory notes to the Bill state (at para.178) that s.60(2) "provides a definition of the term 'sexual' where it is used in the Bill", but that is not in fact what s.60(2) says.

[24] Defined in s.10(1) of the 2009 Act: see below, para.2.42.

[25] Historically, this was also true of academic discussions. For a striking example, see the commentary on the Model Penal Code, where it is asserted that: "Evidentiary considerations aside, consent appears to be a conceptually simple issue. Either the female assented to intercourse, or she did not." (American Law Institute, *Model Penal Code and Commentaries Part II §§210.0 to 213.6* (Philadelphia: American Law Institute, 1980), p.302). See now such detailed commentaries as Alan Wertheimer, *Consent to Sexual Relations* (Cambridge: Cambridge University Press, 2003) and Peter Westen, *The Logic of Consent* (Aldershot: Ashgate, 2004).

[26] *Marr (Brian Knowles) v HM Advocate*, 1996 S.C.C.R. 696.

[27] *Marr v HM Advocate*, 1996 S.C.C.R. 696 at 699.

evant rules were sketchy at best.[28] Although there was some reference in *Lord Advocate's Reference (No.1 of 2001)*[29] to consent as "active consent", there was little discussion of just what the word "active" might mean in this context. Its use appeared to be exegetical, highlighting the fact that, "mere submission or permission" did not amount to "consent".[30]

The Scottish Law Commission considered this position to be unsatisfactory:

> "If consent is to be a central part of the law, then the law should provide guidance as to what the term means".[31]

The definition suggested by the Commission, and which is consequently used in the 2009 Act, is "free agreement",[32] a term taken from the law applicable in the Australian state of Victoria.[33]

The meaning of "free agreement"

1.04 "Free agreement" is not itself defined further by the 2009 Act,[34] although the Commission referred approvingly to statutory jury directions found in Victoria, suggesting that similar (non-statutory) directions could be developed for use in Scotland.[35] As the Victorian legislation currently stands, it requires the judge to (unless it is not relevant to the facts in issue in the proceeding) direct the jury[36]:

> "... that the fact that a person did not say or do anything to indicate free agreement to a sexual act at the time at which the act took place is enough to show that the act took place without that person's free agreement ..."

and

> "... that the jury is not to regard a person as having freely agreed to a sexual act just because—
> (i)   she or he did not protest or physically resist; or
> (ii)   she or he did not sustain physical injury; or
> (iii)   on that or an earlier occasion, she or he freely agreed to engage in another sexual act (whether or not of the same type) with that person, or a sexual act with another person".

Subject to relatively minor glosses such as these, it is doubtful that a judge should go any further—subject to the special cases noted below—in explaining to a jury what is meant by "free agreement".[37] The words of Lord Goddard

---

[28]   See Gordon, *Criminal Law*, para.33.05 and below, paras 1.10–1.11.

[29]   *Lord Advocate's Reference (No.1 of 2001)*, 2002 S.L.T. 466.

[30]   See *Lord Advocate's Reference (No.1 of 2001)*, 2002 S.L.T. 466, per the Lord Justice-General (Cullen) at [46]; cf. *R. v Olugboja (Stephen)* [1982] Q.B. 320, per Dunn L.J. at 332, where it was said that, in accordance with consent's "ordinary meaning", "there is a difference between consent and submission; every consent involves a submission, but it by no means follows that a mere submission involves consent".

[31]   *Report*, para.2.5.

[32]   *Report*, paras 2.36–2.42; 2009 Act s.12.

[33]   Crimes Act 1958 (Vic) s.36, as amended.

[34]   There are, however, provisions in s.15 stating explicitly that, "[c]onsent to conduct does not of itself imply consent to any other conduct" and addressing withdrawal of consent. On the latter point, see below, para.1.05.

[35]   *Report*, para.2.33.

[36]   Crimes Act 1958 (Vic) ss.37, 37AAA, as amended. The provisions quoted are s.37AAA(d), (e).

[37]   Research may be required, however, to establish properly just how "free agreement" is understood by juries, and to develop further glosses if required. See further Emily Finch and Vanessa E. Munro, "Breaking Boundaries? Sexual Consent in the Jury Room" (2006) 26 L.S. 303.

C.J. in *R. v Spriggs*, a case decided shortly after the Scottish defence of diminished responsibility was incorporated into English law by s.2 of the Homicide Act 1957, are instructive[38]:

> "... a judge dealing with this matter can do [no] more than to call the attention of the jury to the exact terms of the section which Parliament has enacted and leave them to say whether upon the evidence they are satisfied that the case comes within the section or not. When Parliament has defined a particular state of things, as they have defined here what is to amount to diminished responsibility, it is not for judges to re-define or to attempt to define the definition. The definition has been laid down by Parliament and it is a question then for the jury. It is a question of fact in any particular case as to whether the jury find that the defendant's evidence brings him within the section or whether it does not."

Withdrawal of consent

Section 15 of the 2009 Act confirms, if there were any doubt, that consent to **1.05** conduct may be withdrawn at any time before or during conduct, and that if conduct takes place, or continues to take place, thereafter, it takes place without consent.[39]

Special cases

The 2009 Act does go beyond the general "free agreement" definition in a **1.06** number of instances. First, under s.12, it lists six cases where consent takes place without free agreement. The model employed is similar to that found in England, but differs in that the English rules are expressed as a mixture of conclusive and rebuttable presumptions,[40] whereas the Scottish Law Commission recognised that these should not properly be understood as "presumptions" at all: they are factors which are in themselves constitutive of a lack of consent.[41] Secondly, s.13 makes special provision for cases where the complainer is asleep or unconscious. Thirdly, s.17 makes special provision for consent by mentally disordered persons. Each of these special rules will be considered in turn.

Alcohol and other intoxicants[42]

Section 13(2)(a) of the 2009 Act provides that free agreement is absent: **1.07**

> "... where the conduct occurs at a time when B is incapable because of the effect of alcohol or any other substance of consenting to it".

The cause of B's incapacity is irrelevant: in this respect, the 2009 Act differs from the pre-2002 position whereby sexual intercourse with a drugged woman could only be rape under Scots law if the accused or an accomplice had drugged the woman for this purpose.[43] Such cases could, however, have

---

[38]   *R. v Spriggs (John Francis)* [1958] 1 Q.B. 270 at 274.
[39]   See *Report*, paras 2.85, 2.86 and *Kaitamaki v The Queen* [1985] A.C. 147.
[40]   Sexual Offences Act 2003 ss.75, 76.
[41]   *Report*, para.2.46.
[42]   See S. Cowan, "The Trouble with Drink: Intoxication, (In)capacity, and the Evaporation of Consent to Sex" (2008) 41 Akron L.R. 899; Philip N.S. Rumney and Rachel Anne Fenton, "Intoxicated Consent in Rape: *Bree* and Juror Decision-Making" (2008) 71 M.L.R. 279.
[43]   *HM Advocate v Logan (David Young)*, 1936 J.C. 100; *HM Advocate v Grainger (Samuel)*, 1932 J.C. 40. This followed because the accused had not "overcome the will" of the victim. Sexual intercourse with a woman who was incapacitated at her own hand or that of a third party would have been clandestine injury.

been rape in Scots law following the decision in *Lord Advocate's Reference (No.1 of 2001).*[44]

The Commission took the view that it was impossible to, "set a test for when a person lacks capacity to consent as a consequence of taking drink or drugs"[45]: the matter is one for the jury. Capacity should not, however, be confused with consciousness: the first may be lost well before the second.[46] It has been said that, "drunken consent is still consent",[47] but such a phrase is best avoided because it obscures the crucial issue, which is whether B in fact had the capacity to consent.[48] The relevant question is B's capacity at the time of intercourse: the fact that B may have contributed to his or her own loss of capacity is irrelevant. This is a particularly important point given research evidence to the effect that juries may be inclined improperly to ascribe responsibility for intercourse to intoxicated victims.[49]

Violence or the threat of violence

1.08 Section 13(2)(b) of the 2009 Act provides that free agreement is absent:

> "... where B agrees or submits to the conduct because of violence used against B or any other person, or because of threats of violence made against B or any other person".

On its face this adds little to the common law,[50] but a number of points are significant. First, the violence need not immediately precede the sexual activity, meaning that it could cover, "what is known as historic abuse".[51] Secondly, it makes it clear that the threat or violence can be against a person other than B, and that A need not be personally responsible for that threat or violence.

Some of these cases, however, may be difficult to pursue to conviction in practice: first because of the difficulty of proving a causal link between the violence and B's agreement or submission, and secondly because where a third party is responsible, A's lack of knowledge may mean that he lacks the degree of fault necessary to be convicted of the crime. If, for example, B is coerced into prostitution by threats of violence from C and A pays B for sexual intercourse, s.13(2)(b) will mean that there is no valid consent on B's part. However, if A were ignorant of the surrounding circumstances and reasonably believed that B consented, he would not be guilty of rape.[52] C would be guilty of sexual coercion under s.4 of the 2009 Act.[53]

---

[44] *Lord Advocate's Reference (No.1 of 2001)*, 2002 S.L.T. 466. See below, para.2.02.

[45] *Report*, para.2.63.

[46] *R. v Bree (Benjamin)* [2007] EWCA Crim 804; [2008] Q.B. 131, per Sir Igor Judge (President, QB) at [34].

[47] *R. v Bree* [2008] Q.B. 131, per Sir Igor Judge (President, QB) at [32], where it is admitted that, "the phrase lacks delicacy".

[48] See Andrew Ashworth's comment on *Bree* at [2007] Crim. L.R. 900.

[49] See Emily Finch and Vanessa E. Munro, "Juror Stereotypes and Blame Attribution in Rape Cases Involving Intoxicants: The Findings of a Pilot Study" (2005) Brit. J. Criminol. 25; Emily Finch and Vanessa E. Munro, "The Demon Drink and the Demonized Woman: Socio-Sexual Stereotypes and Responsibility Attribution in Rape Trials Involving Intoxicants" (2007) 16 S. & L.S. 591.

[50] See Hume, i, 302: "It is evidently no consent, to do away the guilt of rape, if the woman only discontinue her resistance out of fear of death, as when a pistol is clapped to her head, or a dagger to her breast; or if she be threatened with destruction, and so beaten and abused, as to alarm her for her life."

[51] *Report*, para.2.68.

[52] 2009 Act s.1(1)(b). Under English law, by contrast, A would now be guilty of an offence of paying for sexual services of a prostitute subject to force: Sexual Offences Act 2003 s.53A, as inserted by s.14 of the Policing and Crime Act 2009. A's lack of awareness of C's actions would be irrelevant: see 2003 Act s.53A(2)(b).

[53] See below, para.2.15.

Unlawful detention

Section 13(2)(c) of the 2009 Act provides that free agreement is absent, "where **1.09**
B agrees or submits to the conduct because B is unlawfully detained by A".
The Scottish Law Commission suggested that this could go so far as to apply
to "Stockholm syndrome" cases where a victim becomes emotionally attached
to a captor.[54] It is not clear why this provision does not extend (in contrast to
the provisions on violence) to cases where B is unlawfully detained by a third
party, but s.13(2)(c) would not preclude the jury from holding that consent was
similarly absent in such a case.

Deceit as to the nature or purpose of the act[55]

Section 13(2)(d) of the 2009 Act provides that free agreement is absent: **1.10**

"… where B agrees or submits to the conduct because B is mistaken, as a
result of deception by A, as to the nature or purpose of the conduct".

The position at common law in such cases was unclear: there was no directly relevant Scottish authority and discussions in the Scottish textbooks were
generally restricted to English cases which held that a fraud by A as to the
nature of the act invalidated consent.[56] Such circumstances might arise where,
for example, A misled B into thinking that what was proposed was a medical procedure[57]: a plausible misrepresentation in the nineteenth or even early
twentieth century perhaps, particularly where the complainer was young, but
less likely in modern society.[58] Such cases do not really involve a "negation" of
consent: although B has consented to *something*, there is no consent *to sexual
intercourse*.[59]

Frauds as to purpose are a different matter: here, B is aware of the sexual
nature of the act but believes that it is, for example, necessary for medical
reasons. Courts in common law jurisdictions have tended to hold that such a
fraud does not invalidate consent,[60] but the 2009 Act clearly departs from that
position. This is to some extent uncontroversial, and the Scottish Law Commission's reasoning seems to have been that there were certain frauds which
a narrow conception of "nature of the act" might potentially, but improperly,
exclude[61]: for example, if B understands that the act which A wishes to perform
involves the insertion of A's penis into her vagina, it might be argued that she
is perfectly well aware of the nature of the act even if she does not understand
it to be a sexual one. The inclusion of frauds as to purpose in s.13(2)(d) avoids
this problem, but it is not clear that all frauds as to purpose should negate consent: for example, if A and B have sexual intercourse, which B believes is for

---

[54] *Report*, para.2.72.

[55] See generally Jonathan Herring, "Mistaken Sex" [2005] Crim. L.R. 511; P.J. Falk, "Rape by
Fraud and Rape by Coercion" (1998) 64 Brooklyn L.R. 39.

[56] See, e.g. Gordon, *Criminal Law*, para.33.05; R.A.A. McCall Smith and David Sheldon, *Scots
Criminal Law*, 2nd edn (Edinburgh: Butterworths, 1997), p.200.

[57] See *R. v Case (William)* (1850) 4 Cox C.C. 220; *R. v Flattery (John)* (1887) 13 Cox C.C. 388;
R. v Williams (Owen Richard) [1923] 1 K.B. 340.

[58] But still potentially possible in some cases of e.g. youth and/or mental impairment.

[59] See *R. v Clarence (Charles James)* (1889) L.R. 22 Q.B.D. 23, per Stephen J. at 44. Therefore,
if A does not disclose to B that he has a sexually transmitted infection such as HIV, this does not
change the nature of the act—it remains sexual intercourse—and B's consent is not negated. See
R. v B [2006] EWCA Crim 2945; [2007] 1 W.L.R. 1567. A may, however, be guilty of a separate
criminal offence in respect of any transmission of infection which occurs, or exposure to such
transmission. See James Chalmers, "Sexually Transmitted Diseases and the Criminal Law", 2001
Jur. Rev. 259.

[60] See, e.g. *Bolduc and Bird v R.* (1967) 63 D.L.R. (2d) 82; *R. v Mobilio* [1991] 1 V.R. 339; cf.
however, *R. v Harms* [1944] 1 W.W.R. 12.

[61] See *Report*, para.2.73.

the purpose of procreation, but A does not reveal to B that he is infertile, should this amount to rape?[62]

One difficulty, not addressed in the 2009 Act itself or the Scottish Law Commission's report, is the issue of concurrent purposes. In *R. v Linekar*,[63] it was held that where A made a false promise of payment to a prostitute to induce her to consent to sexual intercourse with him, this was not a fraud as to the nature of the act (as English law would then have required for consent to be negated). But is it a fraud as to purpose? One English textbook asserts that it is not: "... clearly A's purpose was sexual gratification and B's purpose was to provide it".[64] But B's purpose might equally be characterised as "to earn money".[65] It may be that frauds as to purposes which are in some way ancillary do not negate consent,[66] but there is no clear basis in the legislation for any such approach.

It will be noted that there must be deception on the part of A in order for s.13(2)(d) to operate. This does not preclude a jury holding that free agreement is absent in other cases: the fact that B's mistake is unilateral or induced by a third party is not a license for A to exploit it.[67]

Impersonation

1.11 Section 13(2)(e) of the 2009 Act provides that free agreement is absent:

"... where B agrees or submits to the conduct because A induces B to agree or submit to the conduct by impersonating a person known personally to B".

At common law, the leading case is *William Fraser*,[68] where it was held that Fraser had not committed rape by impersonating a woman's husband in order to have sexual intercourse with her. The point had arisen elsewhere in the United Kingdom, and legislation was passed declaring it to be rape to obtain sexual intercourse with a married woman in this way.[69] The English courts held that the provision was merely declaratory and did not preclude the courts from recognising that other frauds as to identity (as where A impersonated B's boyfriend) could invalidate consent.[70] Section 13(2)(e) effectively broadens the earlier statutory provision in this way. It does not, however, encompass status frauds such as a false representation from A that he is married to B.[71]

The provision is unsatisfactorily limited to deceit on the part of A. *Allan v HM Advocate*[72] demonstrates the difficulty with this: here, the accused had

---

[62]   See Mitchell C. Davies, "Consenting to Battery Under a Misapprehension: Mistake as to Quality in the Court of Appeal" (2002) 31 C.L.W.R. 236, 247.

[63]   *R. v Linekar (Gareth)* [1995] Q.B. 250.

[64]   Card, Gillespie and Hirst, *Sexual Offences*, para.3.46.

[65]   Card, Gillespie and Hirst, *Sexual Offences*, seem to suggest that this is a "motive" rather than a "purpose", but the distinction is hardly a clear one.

[66]   See also Rook and Ward, *Sexual Offences*, para.1.147, who discuss the case of a gynaecologist who truthfully tells a patient that an intimate medical examination is necessary but with a secondary purpose of obtaining sexual gratification from the examination, and conclude that consent would (under the equivalent English legislation) be negated in such a case.

[67]   See e.g. *Papadimitropoulos v The Queen* (1957) 98 C.L.R. 249 at 260; Law Commission, *Consent in Sex Offences: A Report to the Home Office Sex Offences Review* (The Stationery Office, 2000), para.5.50.

[68]   *William Fraser* (1847) Ark. 280.

[69]   See the Criminal Law (Consolidation) (Scotland) Act 1995 s.7(3), which derives from the Criminal Law Amendment Act 1885 s.4.

[70]   *R. v Elbekkay* [1995] Crim. L.R. 163.

[71]   As arose on the facts of *Gray v Criminal Injuries Compensation Board*, 1993 S.L.T. 28 (bigamous marriage) and *Papadimitropoulos v The Queen* (1957) 98 C.L.R. 249 (false representation that an application for a marriage license had constituted a marriage ceremony).

[72]   *Allan v HM Advocate*, 2004 S.C.C.R. 278. See James Chalmers, "Fraud, Mistake and Consent in Rape: Some Preliminary Observations", 2006 S.L.T. (News) 29.

entered the complainer's hotel room uninvited and penetrated her, "whilst she was under the mistaken belief that" he was her boyfriend. There is nothing in the indictment which suggests that the accused had engaged in actual deception, nor indeed that he was even aware that the complainer had a boyfriend.[73] Yet, despite that, there are good reasons to regard a charge of rape in such circumstances as relevant. The facts are redolent of an actor who simply does not care about the consent of the other party. In such a case, it should be open to the jury to hold that consent was absent, although this would be on the basis of the general test of "free agreement" rather than s.13(2)(e) itself.

Indication of consent from third party

Section 13(2)(e) of the 2009 Act provides that free agreement is absent, "where **1.12** the only expression or indication of agreement to the conduct is from a person other than B". The Scottish Law Commission acknowledged that it, "might be thought that such a provision is unnecessary and does no more than state the obvious".[74]

Consent and the sleeping complainer

The Scottish Law Commission proposed that the list of scenarios where con- **1.13** sent was specified to be absent should include cases:

> "… where the person had taken or been given alcohol or other substances and as a result lacked the capacity to consent at the time of expressing or indicating consent unless consent had earlier been given to engaging in the activity in that condition".[75]

This proved controversial as the Bill was progressing through Parliament, with the suggestion being made that it was difficult to see when an individual would wish to give such consent[76] and that the rule might, "make it easier for men to get away with rape".[77] Such criticisms are internally inconsistent: it is not clear why, if a claim of prior consent in such cases were implausible, a properly directed jury would accept it.

In response to these criticisms, the Scottish Government amended the Bill to include instead the provision that, "[a] person is incapable, while asleep or unconscious, of consenting to any conduct".[78] The meaning of this provision is unclear and the lack of clarity may indeed have been necessary in order to secure Parliamentary agreement. It has two possible meanings. The first is that any conduct which takes place when B is asleep is necessarily non-consensual. Beyond the fact that it is not obvious why the law should bar B from giving consent to sexual activity while asleep if B so desires, the more serious difficulty with this approach is that the Bill is not concerned merely with sexual intercourse, but with all sexual activity. On this reading, it could be a criminal offence for A to wake B with a kiss, even if they had been happily married for

---

[73] In fact, there was another man—not the complainer's boyfriend, but a friend of the couple—asleep in a chair in the room, so it is not beyond the bounds of possibility that the accused assumed him to be the complainer's boyfriend and was impersonating the wrong person.

[74] *Report*, para.2.78.

[75] *Report*, para.2.59.

[76] See the written evidence submitted to the Justice Committee by the Equality and Human Rights Commission Scotland (para.3.1) and by Professor Michele Burman (para.4.6), which adopt very similar language. The written evidence submitted to the Committee is available at *http://www.scottish.parliament.uk/s3/committees/justice/inquiries/SexualOffences/sexualoffencessubmissions.htm* [Accessed May, 22 2010].

[77] Paragraph 4.2 of the written evidence of Rape Crisis Scotland. See also the extensive critique provided in s.1 of Professor Jennifer Temkin's written evidence.

[78] 2009 Act s.14(2).

decades, as it would be impossible to draw any inference of consent from the surrounding circumstances. The better approach seems to be to interpret the statutory provision as meaning that a person who is asleep or unconscious cannot give consent while in that state, in which case the possibility of them giving consent at an earlier stage is not excluded. That is supported by the language used by the Cabinet Secretary for Justice in moving the relevant amendment.[79]

Consent and mental disorder

1.14 With the exception of the offence of sexual abuse of trust of a mentally disordered person,[80] the 2009 Act does not create separate offences relating to sexual activity with persons with a mental disorder.[81] Instead, the general sexual offences apply and special provision is made relating to the capacity of mentally disordered persons to consent. Section 17(2) is the following terms[82]:

> "A mentally disordered person is incapable of consenting to conduct where, by reason of mental disorder, the person is unable to do one or more of the following—
> (a)   understand what the conduct is,
> (b)   form a decision as to whether to engage in the conduct (or as to whether the conduct should take place),
> (c)   communicate any such decision."

For these purposes, "the conduct" must be understood as the specific conduct in question.[83] This provision adds little if anything to the general law: if a person has one of the inabilities specified in the section for a reason *other* than mental disorder, then they would seem to be equally incapable of consenting to conduct. Whether the inability arises from mental disorder or otherwise, its presence can mean no more than that the actus reus of the offence has been established: it will still be necessary to show that A had no reasonable belief that B consented.

CONSENT AND THE AGE OF THE COMPLAINER

1.15 In discussing sexual offences, it is common to refer to the "age of consent", although the Scottish Law Commission rightly pointed out that the law is rather more nuanced than that term might suggest.[84] Although the age of consent in Scotland is commonly—and legitimately—understood at 16, this being the age at which individuals can normally give full and valid consent to sexual contact, no single age of consent actually exists at law. A distinction is drawn, for example, between the age below which a child cannot give a valid consent and the age below which a child can give no consent at all. For that reason, sexual intercourse with a girl under the age of 16 is a criminal offence,[85] but

---

[79]   See James Chalmers, "Two Problems in the Sexual Offences (Scotland) Bill", 2009 S.C.L. 553, where the issue is discussed in more detail.

[80]   2009 Act s.46. See below, para.2.55.

[81]   In contrast to the approach found in England under the Sexual Offences Act 2003 ss.30–44. See Gerry Maher, "Rape and Other Things: Sexual Offences and People with Mental Disorder" (2010) 14 Edin. L.R. 129. Section 311 of the Mental Health (Care and Treatment) (Scotland) Act 2003 (non-consensual acts with or towards mentally disordered persons) is repealed by the 2009 Act.

[82]   This section applies only to the offences under ss.1–9 of the 2009 Act, consent being irrelevant to the other offences which the Act creates. "Mental disorder" has the same meaning as in s.328 of the Mental Health (Care and Treatment) (Scotland) Act 2003: see 2009 Act s.17(1).

[83]   See *R. v C* [2009] UKHL 42; [2009] 1 W.L.R. 1786, per Baroness Hale of Richmond at [27]: "… it is difficult to think of an activity which is more person- and situation-specific than sexual relations. One does not consent to sex in general. One consents to this act of sex with this person at this time and in this place."

[84]   *Report*, para.4.18.

[85]   Having intercourse with an older child: 2009 Act s.28.

cannot be rape unless the absence of factual consent is specifically proven.[86] Sexual activity with a child of that age is necessarily criminal, but the existence of consent will mean that it is the less serious of two possible offences. By contrast, sexual intercourse with a girl under the age of 13 is rape regardless of anything which might be described as factual consent.[87] Different ages may apply in other contexts, such as the offence of sexual abuse of trust which makes it an offence for A to engage in a sexual activity with B where A is in a position of trust in relation to B and B is under the age of 18.[88]

The 2009 Act retains the general rule that fully valid sexual consent can only be given when B reaches the age of 16,[89] and establishes a rule that consent is deemed to be impossible where B is below the age of 13. This is a rationalisation of the previous rules which formerly set that age at either 12 or 13 depending on the particular offence involved.[90]

The concept of older and younger children

On this basis, the scheme of the 2009 Act involves a distinction between **1.16** "young children" and "older children". These terms are not defined in any overarching provision but instead specifically in relation to each offence. The definitions are, however, consistent. A young child is someone who has not yet attained the age of 13 years; an older child is someone who has attained the age of 13 years but not the age of 16. Many of the offences created in the first part of the Act (rape, etc.) are consequently mirrored by related offences in respect of both older and younger children, and these variants of offences are grouped together throughout this book as appropriate.[91]

Sexual activity between children

The Scottish Law Commission recommended that sexual offences against **1.17** older children should be incapable of commission by a person who had not reached the age of 16.[92] Accordingly, consensual sexual activity between older children would not have been subject to the criminal law, although the Commission recommended that the fact that a child had engaged in (or been subjected to) sexual activity with another person should be a ground of referral to a children's hearing.[93] This would not have rendered older children immune from prosecution for sexual offences: they would have remained liable to prosecution for any of the general, non age-specific offences, as well as for any sexual offence against a younger child.

---

[86] In which case it could amount to rape under s.1 of the 2009 Act.

[87] Under the 2009 Act, this is the offence of rape of a young child: s.18. At common law, the relevant age was 12 rather than 13, the rule being that the absence of consent, "should ... be presumed" where the complainer was under that age: *Lord Advocate's Reference (No.1 of 2001)*, 2002 S.L.T. 466, per the Lord Justice-General (Cullen) at [44].

[88] 2009 Act s.42. See below, para.2.51. See also the offence of intercourse with a step-child under s.2 of the Criminal Law (Consolidation) (Scotland) Act 1995, which effectively places the "age of consent" for such conduct at 21 (and bars it for all time where at any time before attaining the age of 18 years had lived in the same household and been treated as a child of the accused's family).

[89] Although this is not an exact replication of the pre-Act position, as a boy over the age of 14 could formerly consent to heterosexual sexual activity: see James Chalmers, "Sexual Offences in Scotland: An Agenda for Reform", 2004 S.L.T. (News) 109.

[90] So the age was 12 for the offence of rape (see above, fn.87) but there was also a statutory offence of sexual intercourse with a girl under the age of 13, where consent was irrelevant and a convicted person liable to life imprisonment: Criminal Law (Consolidation) (Scotland) Act 1995 s.5(1).

[91] A table of equivalencies can be found in Brown, *Sexual Offences (Scotland) Act 2009*, pp.3, 4.

[92] *Report*, para.4.55.

[93] *Report*, para.4.56.

A strong argument in favour of this approach is that it reflects reality: children are rarely if ever prosecuted for consensual sexual activity and legislatures should not pass laws which they are not prepared to enforce. However, the Scottish Government did not accept the Commission's recommendation in full,[94] and so the 2009 Act includes offences of older children engaging in sexual conduct with each other.[95] These offences (which are discussed in more detail later in this book)[96] are restricted to more serious sexual contact (penile penetration and oral-genital contact). They therefore avoid in part the "legislative overkill"[97] which is one of the most objectionable features of the Sexual Offences Act 2003 in England and Wales, where any sexual touching (even, potentially, kissing) between children can amount to a criminal offence.[98]

The result of all of this is that the concept of the "age of consent", which is likely to continue to be commonly understood as 16, becomes even more complicated. Effectively, once a child becomes 13 they can consent to sexual activity short of the actions specified in s.37 provided that their partner is also an older child. Once one of these two parties turns 16 their activities will continue to be lawful if they are two years or less apart in age, in which case the proximity of age defence[99] will apply. Generally, the activities which are excluded from the proximity of age defence are broadly identical to those criminalised under s.37 when both A and B are older children. Once both A and B turn 16, they are free to engage in consensual sexual conduct without these restrictions. These rules certainly reflect better the nature of passage into adulthood than does a binary "age of consent", but they have the consequential (and perhaps inevitable) demerit of being unlikely to be widely understood by the general public.

The drafting does not, however, ensure exact symmetry between the actions which older children can lawfully engage in and those which are excluded from the proximity of age defence. It is lawful for two older children to emit urine or saliva on to each other sexually while they remain children,[100] but as the proximity of age defence (discussed in the next paragraph) is excluded in relation to this form of sexual activity,[101] such behaviour would become a criminal offence on the part of A as soon as A turned 16 and for so long as B remained a child, regardless of how narrow the age gap between A and B was.

Proximity of age defence

1.18 Section 39(3) of the 2009 Act creates a proximity of age defence to most sexual offences against older children. If the difference between A's age and B's age does not exceed two years,[102] the defence applies. Its ambit is, however, limited in respect of the offence of engaging in sexual activity with or towards an older child (s.30), where it is restricted so as not to cover a list of actions at what might be regarded as the more serious end of the spectrum.[103] The de-

---

[94] See *Policy Memorandum*, paras 110–122.

[95] 2009 Act s.37.

[96] See below, para.2.49.

[97] Spencer, "The Sexual Offences Act 2003: (2) Child and Family Offences" [2004] Crim. L.R. 347, 354.

[98] Sexual Offences Act 2003 ss.9, 13.

[99] See below, para.1.18.

[100] Because it is not one of the "things" specified in s.37(3) of the 2009 Act.

[101] See 2009 Act s.39(4), where s.30(2)(e) is not one of the offences listed as being subject to the defence.

[102] This differs from the rather convoluted Commission proposals whereby the defence would have depended on age expressed in whole years with a defence of prior sexual conduct to deal with the fact that such a difference might vary over time between two and three years: *Report*, paras 4.75–4.78.

[103] See below, para.2.47.

fence is also inapplicable to the offences of older children engaging in sexual conduct with each other (s.37), but these offences are similarly, although not identically, restricted to more serious sexual conduct (here, penile penetration and oral-genital contact).[104] The defence is therefore relevant only where A is over the age of 16, as the offences against older children other than those under s.37 cannot in any event be committed where A is below that age.

Mistaken beliefs as to age

The 2009 Act deals with mistakes by A as to B's age in the following way: **1.19**

Mistaken belief as to the age of a younger child

Under s.27 of the Act, it is never a defence to an offence against a young **1.20** child—that is, an offence under ss.18–26—that A believed that B had attained the age of 13 years.

This rule, while normally unproblematic, may cause difficulties where A is also a child, as demonstrated by the House of Lords decision in *R. v G*,[105] concerning the equivalent rule in English law. There, A, a 15-year-old boy, had sexual intercourse with B, a 12-year-old girl. B claimed not to have consented; A claimed that she had consented and that he had believed her to be 15 years of age. A was charged with the rape of a young child[106] and the prosecution accepted a plea of guilty on the basis of A's account of events.

The House of Lords upheld the conviction, holding unanimously that the imposition of strict liability was compatible with art.6 of the European Convention on Human Rights. Two of the five judges, however (Lord Hope of Craighead and Lord Carswell) concluded that the prosecution had breached the defendant's rights under art.8, taking the view that the Crown—having decided to proceed on the basis of A's account—should have, as a discretionary matter, substituted a charge under s.13 of the Sexual Offences Act 2003 ("child sex offences committed by children or young persons").[107] The majority rejected that contention and upheld G's conviction.

The difficulty with the prosecution in *R. v G* is this. The normal rule of strict liability in such cases is easily justified on the basis that if B is under 13, A could not conceivably believe that B is in fact 16 or older. By engaging in sexual activity with B, A therefore knows that he is committing a criminal offence: if the offence turns out to be more serious than he realised, that is simply a risk he has chosen to take and he cannot rely on his mistake as a defence.[108] Put differently, his mistake is deemed to be irrelevant. But the situation is in reality different when A is himself a child. Consensual sexual intercourse between two 15 year olds is unlikely to be the subject of criminal prosecution, and indeed would not have been prosecutable under the 2009 Act had the Scottish Law Commission's recommendations on this point been accepted.[109] On the facts accepted by the prosecution in *R. v G*, therefore, it is difficult to regard A's mistake as truly irrelevant. While the exercise of prosecutorial discretion might be appropriate in such cases, the structure of the 2009 Act means that there is no obvious appropriate alternative offence. A could perhaps be charged under s.37 with attempting to engage in sexual conduct with an older child, but

---

[104] See below, para.2.49.

[105] *R. v G* [2008] UKHL 37; [2009] 1 A.C. 92.

[106] Under s.5 of the Sexual Offences Act 2003. In Scotland, see s.18 of the 2009 Act.

[107] This provision makes it an offence for a person under 18 to do anything which would be an offence under any of ss.9–12 of the 2003 Act if he were 18.

[108] See *R. v G* [2009] 1 A.C. 92, per Baroness Hale of Richmond at [46]. See also Jeremy Horder, "How Culpability Can, and Cannot, Be Denied in Under-age Sex Crimes" [2001] Crim. L.R. 15.

[109] See above, para.1.17. The Commission did not, however, discuss whether this had any consequences for the imposition of strict liability as to the age of a young child.

that is open to the objection that it obscures the reality of sexual intercourse having actually taken place.[110]

Mistaken belief as to the age of an older child

1.21 It is never a defence to an offence against an older child—that is, an offence under ss.28–37—that A believed B was in fact a young child.[111] It is a defence under s.39(1) that A, "reasonably believed that B had attained the age of 16 years". The accused bears only an evidential burden in respect of this defence.[112]

"Reasonable belief" is not defined, although there is authority (dealing with analogous provisions in earlier legislation)[113] to the effect that it is not sufficient for this to be based on B's appearance alone,[114] unless perhaps B has some, "extraordinary development of body and mental power".[115] Nor, it seems, is B's claim to be 16 years old sufficient, unless it is corroborated by friends,[116] family,[117] some form of proof of age[118] or circumstances such as B's presence in a venue to which only adults should be admitted.[119] While B's appearance in the witness box may be a factor to be taken into account, it would be wrong for the judge or jury simply to substitute their own view of B's apparent age for that of A. It is possible that the reasonableness of A's belief may be affected by characteristics of his own such as mental disorder or low intelligence which would affect his ability to appreciate B's correct age.[120]

Restrictions on the availability of the defence of mistaken belief as to the age of an older child

1.22 Under the former statutory offence of intercourse with a girl under 16, the defence that A reasonably believed B was over 16 was only available where A was:

> "... a man under the age of 24 years who had not previously been charged with a like offence [and] had reasonable cause to believe that the girl was of or over the age of 16 years".[121]

This provision (often referred to as the "young man's defence") was an oddity which did not exist in respect of other offences.[122] The Commission rejected the idea that a defence of reasonable mistake should be limited by reference to the accused's age in this way,[123] but suggested that the accused's age could

---

[110] An alternative—and perhaps equally unsatisfactory—approach would be to charge A with the offence of engaging while an older child in sexual conduct with or towards an older child, fictitiously treating B as an older child by relying on the deeming provisions of the 2009 Act (see below, paras 1.31–1.37).

[111] 2009 Act s.39(7).

[112] This is not made explicit in the 2009 Act, but see *Report*, para.4.73.

[113] It has been suggested, however, that the value of such earlier authority may be limited by the fact that the prior legislation referred to, "reasonable cause to believe" rather than, "reasonable belief": Brown, *Sexual Offences (Scotland) Act 2009*, p.67.

[114] *HM Advocate v Macdonald* (1900) 3 Adam 180, per Lord McLaren at 182.

[115] *HM Advocate v Hoggan* (1893) 1 Adam 1, per the Lord Justice-Clerk (Macdonald) at 4.

[116] *Mair v Russell*, 1996 S.C.C.R. 453.

[117] *HM Advocate v Macdonald* (1900) 3 Adam 180.

[118] *HM Advocate v Hoggan* (1893) 1 Adam 1; *Policy Memorandum* para.134.

[119] *Policy Memorandum*, para.134.

[120] See *R. v Hudson (Terence)* [1966] 1 Q.B. 448, per Ashworth J. at 455; Card, Gillespie and Hirst, *Sexual Offences*, para.2.69.

[121] Criminal Law (Consolidation) (Scotland) Act 1995 s.5(5)(b).

[122] Most importantly, indecent behaviour towards a girl between 12 and 16: Criminal Law (Consolidation) (Scotland) Act 1995 s.6.

[123] *Report*, para.4.60

be relevant to the credibility of his claim.[124] (It is not clear why this is so. A judge or jury may, for good reason, be more *sympathetic* to a 16-year-old boy who claims to have made a mistake as to the age of a 15-year-old girl than to a 40-year-old man who claims to have made the same mistake, but that does not mean the former claim is more credible. The opposite may even be true: teenagers are probably better placed to discern the correct age of their contemporaries than middle-aged individuals are.)

However, two limitations, not recommended by the Commission, have been included in the 2009 Act. The s.39(1) defence is not available to A if he has previously been charged by the police with a "relevant sexual offence",[125] or if there is in force in respect of A a risk of sexual harm order.[126] The rationale for these restrictions is not entirely clear,[127] but they can be justified on the basis that a previous charge puts A on special notice as to the rules of the criminal law regarding sexual activity with children.[128] If so, that is only true where the charge pre-dates the activity which forms the basis of the later prosecution, and it is submitted that "previously" should be interpreted accordingly. If A has intercourse with B (who is under 16) in January, is charged with another sexual offence in February, and stands trial in March for sexual intercourse with an older child, the only reason for denying him the s.39(1) defence on the basis of the February charge would be that it in some way demonstrated a propensity to commit the January offence, which seems unfair and irrational.

Matters are more difficult where the Crown seek to bar the defence on the basis of a risk of sexual harm order, because the statutory provision says baldly that the defence is barred when there, "is in force in respect of A" such an order.[129] It seems therefore that the relevant question here is whether the order is in force at the time of the trial, not at the time of the offence. Because such an order requires proof (albeit to the civil standard) of inappropriate sexual behaviour towards a child on at least two occasions,[130] its existence may be rather tenuously regarded a form of character evidence justifying barring of the defence even where the order was granted after the alleged offence. This does have the odd consequence, however, that if there was a risk of sexual harm order in force in respect of A at the time of the offence, but the order has expired by the time A's trial commences, A's right to plead the s.39(1) defence is revived.

---

[124] *Report*, para.4.60. See also *Policy Memorandum*, paras 133, 134.

[125] For a list of these offences, see the 2009 Act Sch.1. In *McMaster (Ross Charles) v HM Advocate*, 2001 S.C.C.R. 517, it was held that a charge of rape meant that the accused should be regarded as a person who had previously been charged with unlawful sexual intercourse with a girl under 16 under s.5(3) of the Criminal Law (Consolidation) Act 1995, that being an available alternative verdict on a charge of rape. The point was important there because the s.5(3) charge was one which barred the accused's right to plead the "young man's defence"; the statute did not explicitly say that a rape charge did so. Whether this approach applies under the differently formulated provisions of the 2009 Act is perhaps arguable (the 2009 Act requires only charge by the police; McMaster had previously been indicted for rape), but the list of offences in Sch.1 of the Act is so extensive as to render the point of marginal importance, if any.

[126] 2009 Act s.39(2).

[127] The Scottish Government asserted that, "removing this restriction [that the accused had not previously been charged with a like offence] could enable serial sexual predators to evade conviction" (*Policy Memorandum*, para.135).

[128] See Christopher H.W. Gane, *Sexual Offences* (Edinburgh: Butterworths, 1992), p.74, who justifies this aspect of the former "young man's defence" on the basis that A has received, "unequivocal notice of the risks involved in having intercourse with young girls" as a result of the former charge. See also *McMaster v HM Advocate*, 2001 S.C.C.R. 517, where Lord Cameron of Lochbroom (at [11]) uses near-identical language to Gane's. Given the point involved in *McMaster* (see above, fn.125) this is surprising: it is not clear that a person charged with rape is in fact given such unequivocal notice.

[129] 2009 Act s.39(2).

[130] Protection of Children and Prevention of Sexual Offences (Scotland) Act 2005 s.2. See also Sexual Offences Act 2003 s.123 in respect of such orders granted elsewhere in the UK.

"WITHOUT ANY REASONABLE BELIEF THAT B CONSENTS"

1.23 At common law, the mens rea of rape (and with it, other sexual offences based on a lack of consent) required that A was reckless as to whether or not B consented.[131] Recklessness, for these purposes, was understood subjectively. It therefore followed that if A believed B to be consenting, A could not be guilty of rape regardless of how unreasonable that belief might be. Sometimes, therefore, the mens rea was expressed in negative terms such as, "the absence of an honest belief on the part of the male that the female is consenting".[132]

This rule was controversial and heavily criticised.[133] It was arguably inconsistent with the general Scottish approach to error of fact and mens rea, where it is sometimes suggested that an error of fact must be reasonable to negate mens rea.[134] In relation to rape itself, there was concern that it could encourage myths regarding sexual behaviour[135] and lead to juries accepting bogus defences.[136] More substantively, it was argued that the rule was wrong in principle: it is easy for A to take steps to ensure that B is consenting, and the law should require him to do so rather than run the risk of non-consent.[137]

The Scottish Law Commission concluded that the common law rule should be replaced by what it described as a "mixed test", requiring reasonable grounds for a belief in consent but still focusing on the accused. Consequently, the offences in Pt 1 of the 2009 Act, all of which are based on a lack of consent, require that A must have acted without any reasonable belief that B consents, and s.16 makes the following provision regarding reasonable belief:

> "In determining, for the purposes of Part 1, whether a person's belief as to consent or knowledge was reasonable, regard is to be had to whether the person took any steps to ascertain whether there was consent or, as the case may be, knowledge; and if so, to what those steps were."

Beyond this, reasonable belief is not defined. The rationale for s.16 requires some explanation. The Commission's starting point was the English statutory provision that:

> "Whether a belief is reasonable is to be determined having regard to all the circumstances, including any steps A has taken to ascertain whether B consents".[138]

The Commission rejected this definition, arguing that it could have the effect of making the test wholly subjective. If the accused's own attributes and belief systems were part of the test, then might it not be said that any belief which he held was one which was reasonable for him to hold?[139]

Section 16 fails to meet that argument, giving only the illusion of an answer

---

[131] *Jamieson (Brian) v HM Advocate*, 1994 J.C. 88; *Meek v HM Advocate*, 1983 S.L.T. 280.

[132] Gordon, *Criminal Law*, para.33.01.

[133] See, e.g. Gane, *Sexual Offences*, 1992, pp.40–45.

[134] On the basis of *Dewar (James) v HM Advocate*, 1945 J.C. 5. The reality is rather more complex. See James Chalmers and Fiona Leverick, *Criminal Defences and Pleas in Bar of Trial* (Edinburgh: W. Green, 2006), Ch.12.

[135] Home Office, *Setting the Boundaries: Reforming the Law on Sex Offences* (The Stationery Office, 2000), Vol.1, para.2.13.7.

[136] Law Commission, *Consent in the Criminal Law* (HMSO, 1995), Law Com C.P. No.139, para.7.12.

[137] See, e.g. Home Office, *Setting the Boundaries*, 2000, Vol.1, para.2.13.7; James Chalmers, "Acquaintance Rape: A Reply", 2000 S.L.T. (News) 163; Home Affairs Committee, *Sexual Offences Bill* (The Stationery Office, 2003), HC Paper No.639 (Session 2002/03), paras 16, 17.

[138] Sexual Offences Act 2003 s.1(2). This rule is repeated throughout relevant offence definitions in the 2003 Act.

[139] The very fact that this would render "reasonable belief" identical to "honest belief" should indicate that the argument is not particularly plausible.

to the problem identified by the Commission. It is no use saying that regard is to be had to something unless it is the only thing that can be taken into account (and it is unlikely that that is what is meant), because it does not answer the more important question: what else can—and cannot—be taken into account?

To take an obvious example: suppose that A were extremely intoxicated at the relevant time. There is no question that this would affect his ability to form accurate beliefs as to whether or not B consented. But is that to be taken into account in deciding whether his belief was reasonable? It is easy not to have sympathy for A on the basis of his intoxication, but what if he was particularly young and immature, or had learning difficulties which affected his ability to assess whether B consented?

In most cases, it should be sufficient for a jury to be directed in accordance with the language of s.16, but it may be necessary in certain circumstances to direct them that certain facts which have been led in evidence are not relevant to that determination. However, the Act provides no guidance on this point. Self-induced intoxication may be an obvious factor which must be left out of account,[140] as might certain beliefs expressed by A about consent to sexual intercourse (for example, if A expressed the view that he was "entitled" to expect sexual intercourse from B for whatever reason). There seems no good reason, however, to disregard factors which do not demonstrate fault or vice on A's part, such as immaturity or learning difficulties.

EXCEPTIONS TO ART AND PART OR INCITEMENT LIABILITY FOR SEXUAL OFFENCES

Sexual offences are subject to the general law as regards art and part liability **1.24** or liability for incitement,[141] but there are two specific situations where special rules apply.

Provision of contraception or sexual health advice to children

Concern may arise as to whether individuals who provide, for example, advice **1.25** on sexual health will be themselves criminally liable if they do so in respect of unlawful activity, such as intercourse where one party is under the age of 16. In *Gillick v West Norfolk and Wisbech Area Health Authority*,[142] the House of Lords held that a doctor who intended to act in the best interests of a girl aged under 16 was either not, or at least unlikely to be, criminally liable as a result of prescribing her contraceptives. The decision was, however, reached by a majority[143] and there was no parallel Scottish authority. The matter is addressed by s.51 of the 2009 Act, which is in the following terms (Pts 4 and 5 of the Act being those headed "Children" and "Abuse of Position of Trust"):

> "A person ('X') is not guilty of inciting, or being involved art and part in, an offence under Part 4 or 5 if, as regards another person ('Y'), X acts—
>> (a)   for the purpose of—
>>> (i)   protecting Y from sexually transmitted infection,
>>> (ii)   protecting the physical safety of Y,
>>> (iii) preventing Y from becoming pregnant, or
>>> (iv)   promoting Y's emotional well-being by the giving of advice, and

---

[140] Which would be consistent with Scots law's general approach to voluntary intoxication: see *Brennan (Ian) v HM Advocate*, 1977 J.C. 38; Chalmers and Leverick, *Criminal Defences and Pleas in Bar of Trial*, 2006, Ch.8.

[141] For which, see Gordon, *Criminal Law*, Chs 5, 6.

[142] *Gillick v West Norfolk and Wisbech AHA* [1986] A.C. 112.

[143] Lords Scarman and Bridge of Harwich thought that the doctor would not be criminally liable; Lord Fraser of Tullybelton that he was unlikely to be. Lords Brandon of Oakbrook and Templeman dissented.

(b) not for the purpose of—
   (i)   obtaining sexual gratification,
   (ii)   humiliating, distressing or alarming Y, or
   (iii) causing or encouraging the activity constituting the offence
          or Y's participation in it."

This provision is modelled on the equivalent English legislation,[144] with the important difference that Y need not (as under English law) be the child against whom the offence is committed. That means, for example, that if X provides a condom to a 15-year-old boy to prevent that boy's 16-year-old girlfriend (Y) becoming pregnant, X falls within the scope of s.51.[145] There is no requirement that X be in any way qualified to provide sexual health or other advice: all that matters is the purpose for which he acts.

Although the aim of the provision appears to be to exclude liability altogether in cases which the Scottish Law Commission described as "counselling",[146] it may be noted that there is no reference to the statutory provision which makes it an offence to aid, abet, counsel, procure or incite an offence against the provisions of any enactment.[147] On the basis of the clear legislative intention disclosed by the Commission's report, and the absence of any authority to the effect that the statutory provision has a broader ambit than the common law,[148] it seems reasonable to conclude that s.51 also excludes liability under this provision.

Victims as parties to sexual offences

1.26 In the leading English case of *R. v Tyrrell*,[149] the defendant—a girl under the age of 16 who had had sexual intercourse with a male person—was charged with aiding and abetting the commission of an offence upon herself and having solicited and incited the commission of that offence upon her. The Court for Crown Cases Reserved held that this fell outwith the relevant statutory offence[150]:

> "… it is impossible to say that the Act, which is absolutely silent about aiding or abetting, or soliciting or inciting, can have intended that the girls for whose protection it was passed should be punishable under it for the offences committed upon themselves".[151]

The rule laid down by this case is probably best understood as one of statutory interpretation: where an offence is created for the protection of a class of persons, it excludes by implication liability on the part of the victim.[152] Such a rule

---

[144] Sexual Offences Act 2003 s.73. For the legislative history of the English provision, see Rook and Ward, *Sexual Offences*, paras 4.103–4.105. One significant change from the 2003 Act's formulation is that, "humiliating, distressing or alarming Y" has been added as a purpose excluding immunity. See *Discussion Paper*, paras 5.77–5.97; *Report*, paras 4.135–4.137. Section 51 is unchanged from s.39 of the Commission's draft Bill: *Report*, p.173.

[145] Which would not be the case in England: see Card, Gillespie and Hirst, *Sexual Offences*, para.2.53.

[146] See *Report*, paras 4.135–4.137.

[147] Criminal Procedure (Scotland) Act 1995 s.292(3).

[148] See Gordon, *Criminal Law*, para.5.12.

[149] *R. v Tyrrell* [1894] 1 Q.B. 710.

[150] Criminal Law Amendment Act 1885 s.5.

[151] *R. v Tyrrell* [1894] 1 Q.B. 710, per Lord Coleridge C.J. at 712.

[152] *Smith and Hogan Criminal Law*, edited by David Ormerod, 12th edn (Oxford: Oxford University Press, 2008), p.230.

is of most significance in respect of sexual offences, but not limited thereto.[153]

Two issues arise: first, is this rule a rule of Scots law and secondly, what is its exact scope? The first question has not been answered by the courts, although it is generally thought that Scots law would adopt such an approach.[154] Presumably if the rule exists as a general principle of statutory interpretation it has not been abrogated by the 2009 Act.[155] But what is its scope?[156] In some cases, this may be obvious—for example, an offence such as that under s.28 ("having intercourse with an older child") is clearly intended to protect the older child, who cannot therefore be guilty of the offence art and part. Something of an oddity arises where both parties are older children, because it then follows that if they have sexual intercourse they are both guilty of an offence under s.37 ("older children engaging in sexual conduct with each other"), but on the day one turns 16 the older party would be guilty of the s.28 offence and the younger party immune from criminal liability.[157] The issue must be one of statutory interpretation to be determined independently in respect of each individual offence, but establishing when an offence is intended to protect a particular class will not always be easy.[158]

RESOLUTION OF TEMPORAL UNCERTAINTY AND UNCERTAINTY AS TO AGE

Temporal uncertainty

One difficulty with statutory reform of the criminal law is that it may in some **1.27** cases be uncertain whether conduct forming the basis of a charge occurred before or after the new law came into force. This problem—referred to here as "temporal uncertainty"—is particularly significant in respect of sexual offences given the lengthy period of time which may elapse between commission and prosecution.[159] After the Sexual Offences Act 2003 came into force in England and Wales on May 1, 2004, a number of prosecutions failed because of uncertainty as to whether the conduct alleged took place before or after that

---

[153] See generally B. Hogan, "Victims as Parties to Crime" [1962] Crim. L.R. 683; G. Williams, "Victims as Parties to Crimes—A Further Comment" [1964] Crim. L.R. 686. Because victims are generally unlikely to be prosecuted as accomplices, the question has arisen more frequently in a prosecution of the principal offender where it is alleged that special rules of evidence should apply to the victim's evidence because of their technical status as an accomplice: see, e.g. *Scott v Killian* (1985) 40 S.A.S.R. 37. Such an argument would no longer be stateable in Scotland given the decision in *Docherty (Andrew) v HM Advocate*, 1987 J.C. 81.

[154] Gordon, *Criminal Law*, para.5.05. See also Gane, *Sexual Offences*, 1992, p.74.

[155] Here, the 2009 Act differs from s.73(3) of the Sexual Offences Act 2003, which expressly preserves the rule for English law: but as the rule is not clearly established in Scots law it might have been difficult for the draughtsman to preserve it expressly.

[156] Although outwith the scope of the 2009 Act, the principle poses particular difficulties in respect of incest, where it has frequently been applied despite the fact that it may not be obvious that the relevant offences are, "intended for the protection of anyone": *Smith and Hogan Criminal Law*, 2008, p.203. See *R. v Whitehouse (Arthur)* [1977] Q.B. 868; *R. v Pickford (John Andrew)* [1995] Q.B. 203. It may also apply in respect of prostitution offences. Here, a woman can be guilty art and part of the offence of living off the earnings of prostitution despite the fact that the statutory provisions refer to, "every male person" who does this committing an offence: Criminal Law (Consolidation) (Scotland) Act 1995 s.11(1) and *Reid (Lindsey) v HM Advocate*, 1999 J.C. 54; but presumably the prostitute herself cannot be guilty: see *R. v Congdon* (1990) 140 N.L.J. 1221.

[157] cf. Michael Bohlander, "The Sexual Offences Act 2003 and the *Tyrrell* principle—Criminalising the Victims?" [2005] Crim. L.R. 701, 711–712.

[158] See Gordon, *Criminal Law*, para.5.05; Glanville Williams, "Victims and Other Exempt Parties in Crime" (1990) 10 L.S. 245, 248.

[159] See, e.g. *HM Advocate v L*, 2009 S.L.T. 127, where charges of incest alleged to have been committed "on various occasions" between 1976 and 1982 called before the High Court in 2007. See also Penney Lewis, *Delayed Prosecution for Childhood Sexual Abuse* (Oxford: Oxford University Press, 2006).

date,[160] even though the conduct in question was criminal under both the old and the new law. The problem was remedied by legislation which the Scottish Law Commission recommended be used as a model for Scots law.[161] The Commission expressed its policy in the following terms[162]:

> "Where the accused is charged with an offence under the Act and with an offence under the law in force prior to the Act, and the actual date on which the accused's conduct took place cannot be proven, the accused is liable to be convicted of an offence under the Act unless the maximum penalty for the offence under the prior law is less than that for the offence under the Act."

The relevant provision—s.53 of the 2009 Act—is expressed in a rather more complicated fashion, but operates as follows. First, it specifies a number of offences which existed prior to the 2009 Act coming into force as "existing offences",[163] offences under the Act being "new offences".[164]

Where there is doubt as to whether conduct took place before or after the 2009 Act came into force, the prosecution should charge the accused with *both* the new offence and the existing offence.[165] If it can be established beyond reasonable doubt that the conduct took place either before or after the 2009 Act came into force, the accused may be convicted of either the existing or new offence as appropriate. If this cannot be established, the accused should be found guilty of the new offence unless the maximum penalty for the existing offence is less than the maximum penalty for the new offence. In such a case, he should be convicted of the existing offence.

In practice, the latter scenario will rarely if ever arise, because the scheme of penalties set up by the 2009 Act does not involve increases in the penalties which were already applicable in respect of the relevant existing offences. This outcome seems possible only in unusual circumstances, such as if A were proven to have had sexual intercourse with B, who was under the age of 16 at the relevant time, and B's consent was valid at common law but invalid under the 2009 Act. In such a case, while B's conduct could amount to rape if it were proven to have taken place after the commencement of the 2009 Act, it will be necessary to convict him under s.5(3) of the Criminal Law (Consolidation) (Scotland) Act 1995 in a case of temporal uncertainty. The same result would obtain if A lacked the mens rea of rape at common law but lacked any reasonable belief that B consented and so satisfied the test set out by s.1(1)(b) of the 2009 Act. This illustrates how cases of temporal uncertainty can require complex directions to be given to the jury setting out two different definitions of what may nominally be the same crime.

---

[160] See *R. v Newbon* [2005] Crim. L.R. 738; *R. v A (Prosecutor's Appeal)* [2005] EWCA Crim 3533; [2006] 1 Cr. App. R. 28; *R. v H (Christopher)* [2006] EWCA Crim 2898. See also *R. v Chaney (David John)* [2009] EWCA Crim 52.

[161] Violent Crime Reduction Act 2006 s.55. See *Report*, paras 7.7–7.10.

[162] *Report*, para.7.10. Section 53 of the 2009 Act is unchanged from s.40 of the Commission's draft Bill (*Report*, pp 174, 175) with the minor addition of s.53(5)(e), applying the section to offences as modified by ss.16A, 16B of the Criminal Law (Consolidation) (Scotland) Act 1995.

[163] 2009 Act s.53(2). These are rape at common law, clandestine injury, lewd, indecent or libidinous practice or behaviour, "any other common law offence which is replaced by an offence under this Act", and offences under the Criminal Law (Consolidation) (Scotland) Act 1995 ss.3, 5, 6, and the Sexual Offences (Amendment) Act 2000 s.3.

[164] For the purposes of s.53, references to offences include attempts, incitement, counselling or procuring, involvement art and part, or offences as modified by the Criminal Law (Consolidation) (Scotland) Act 1995 ss.16A ("Conspiracy or incitement to commit certain sexual acts outside the United Kingdom") and 16B ("Commission of certain sexual acts outside the United Kingdom").

[165] 2009 Act s.53(1)(a). As Brown, *Sexual Offences (Scotland) Act 2009*, p.84 notes, the charges must presumably be in the alternative.

Indecent assault is not an "existing offence" for these purposes, because it continues to exist despite the 2009 Act.[166] Therefore, if, in a case of temporal uncertainty, A has engaged in conduct which would be indecent assault at common law but an offence under the 2009 Act (most obviously, non-consensual anal or oral intercourse), A should be charged with indecent assault. It will not be possible to use s.53 to convict A of rape.

Determining the maximum penalty. The maximum penalty is defined as: **1.28**

"... the maximum penalty by way of imprisonment or other detention that could be imposed on the accused on conviction of the offence in the proceedings in question".[167]

The following table sets this out in respect of each of the statutory "existing offences":

Offence	Maximum penalty
Criminal Law (Consolidation) (Scotland) Act 1995 s.3 (intercourse of person in position of trust with child under 16)	Conviction on indictment: life imprisonment Summary conviction: 12 months' imprisonment[168]
Criminal Law (Consolidation) (Scotland) Act 1995 s.5(1) (unlawful sexual intercourse with girl under 13)	Conviction on indictment: life imprisonment[169]
Criminal Law (Consolidation) (Scotland) Act 1995 s.5(2) (attempt to have unlawful sexual intercourse with girl under 13)	Conviction on indictment: 10 years' imprisonment Summary conviction: 12 months' imprisonment[170]
Criminal Law (Consolidation) (Scotland) Act 1995 s.5(3) (unlawful sexual intercourse with girl over 13 and under 16)	Conviction on indictment: 10 years' imprisonment Summary conviction: 12 months' imprisonment[171]
Criminal Law (Consolidation) (Scotland) Act 1995 s.6 (indecent behaviour towards girl between 12 and 16)	Conviction on indictment: 10 years' imprisonment[172]
Sexual Offences (Amendment) Act 2000 s.3 (abuse of position of trust)	Conviction on indictment: five years' imprisonment Summary conviction: 12 months' imprisonment[173]

---

[166] See below, para.2.13.
[167] 2009 Act s.53(4).
[168] Criminal Law (Consolidation) (Scotland) Act 1995 s.4(5).
[169] Criminal Law (Consolidation) (Scotland) Act 1995 s.5(1).
[170] Criminal Law (Consolidation) (Scotland) Act 1995 s.5(2).
[171] Criminal Law (Consolidation) (Scotland) Act 1995 s.5(3).
[172] Criminal Law (Consolidation) (Scotland) Act 1995 s.6.
[173] Sexual Offences (Amendment) Act 2000 s.3(4).

The offences under ss.5(2), 5(3) and 6 of the Criminal Law (Consolidation) (Scotland) Act 1995 formerly carried maximum penalties of two years' imprisonment, but this was increased to 10 years with effect from August 1, 1997.[174] That change is effectively irrelevant for these purposes given the inherent implausibility of anyone being proved to have committed one of these offences but with a potential 13 year latitude as to the date on which they did so.[175]

The maximum penalty on summary conviction for those offences where summary prosecution was possible was increased to 12 months' imprisonment on December 10, 2007 as a result of the general increase in the sentencing powers of the sheriff in summary procedure.[176] Because this increase had retrospective effect—it did not increase the maximum possible penalty which could be imposed in respect of any offence, but simply allowed penalties of up to 12 months' imprisonment to be imposed in summary rather than solemn procedure[177]—it will always be the 12 month period which is relevant for the purposes of applying s.53 of the 2009 Act.

Temporal uncertainty and mentally disordered complainers

1.29 Not all offences abolished by the Act are specified as "existing offences".[178] A surprising exception in this respect is s.311 of the Mental Health (Care and Treatment) (Scotland) Act 2003, which created an offence of non-consensual sexual acts with or towards a mentally disordered person.[179] The circumstances in which a person would be "regarded as not consenting" where mentally disordered were potentially rather broader than at common law.[180] Under the 2009 Act, this offence no longer exists: instead, special provision is made as regards the capacity of mentally disordered persons to consent,[181] and the general offences then apply.[182] This seems to have the result that where B is mentally disordered, and there is proof that A engaged in sexual activity with B at an uncertain date around the commencement of the 2009 Act, and B's consent would be valid at common law but invalid under s.311 of the 2003 Act and also the 2009 Act, it appears that there is no offence of which A can be convicted. While unsatisfactory, the practical significance of this anomaly is likely to be very limited. The 2009 Act does not replicate the surprisingly broad approach to vitiation of consent found in the 2003 Act—where, most significantly, consent could be invalidated by "persuasion" alone[183]—and cases where B's consent is valid at common law but invalid under the 2009 Act by virtue of its provisions relating to mental disorder are likely to be rare.[184]

---

[174] Crime and Punishment (Scotland) Act 1997 s.14, with the effect of the increase being restricted to offences committed on that date onwards: Crime and Punishment (Scotland) Act 1997 (Commencement and Transitional Provisions) Order 1997 (SI 1997/1712).

[175] In this unlikely event (which might theoretically be possible if B's age at the time of the offence could be proved but her identity could not) it would be necessary to convict of the offence under the 1995 Act on the basis of a maximum penalty of two years' imprisonment.

[176] Criminal Proceedings etc. (Reform) (Scotland) Act 2007 s.45; Criminal Proceedings etc. (Reform) (Scotland) Act 2007 (Commencement No.2 and Transitional Provisions and Savings) Order 2007 (SSI 2007/479). A challenge to the legislative competence of this provision was rejected in *Martin v HM Advocate* [2010] UKSC 10; 2010 S.L.T. 412.

[177] The offence had to be triable either on indictment or summary complaint for the uplift to apply: Criminal Proceedings etc. (Reform) (Scotland) Act 2007 s.45(6)(a).

[178] Most obviously, while the common law offence of sodomy is also abolished by the 2009 Act (s.52(a)(iv)), it is not specified under s.53(2) because it is not replaced by any new offence.

[179] Repealed by 2009 Act Sch.6.

[180] Mental Health (Care and Treatment) (Scotland) Act 2003 s.311(3), (4).

[181] 2009 Act s.17.

[182] For discussion of this scheme, see Maher, "Rape and Other Things" (2010) 14 Edin. L.R. 129.

[183] Mental Health (Care and Treatment) (Scotland) Act 2003 s.311(3)(b)(iv).

[184] And possibly non-existent: see the discussion of s.17 of the 2009 Act above, para.1.14.

Temporal uncertainty and extraterritorial offences

A separate provision—s.56—applies in respect of temporal uncertainty and **1.30** sexual offences committed outside the United Kingdom. There are a number of offences under statutes other than the 2009 Act where individuals can be liable to conviction in Scotland despite having committed the relevant acts outside of the United Kingdom.[185] Prior to the 2009 Act coming into force, the individual would have been convicted of that offence by virtue of s.16B of the Criminal Law (Consolidation) (Scotland) Act 1995; now they would be convicted of that offence by virtue of s.55 of the 2009 Act. In a case of temporal uncertainty, they are to be convicted of the offence "as modified by" s.16B of the 1995 Act.[186] There would seem to be no practical significance in this. The terminology, "as modified by", is peculiar to s.56: the other provisions simply state that the individual has committed the specified offence *itself*, not some variant on it. However, s.56 avoids any possible argument that a conviction is impossible in such cases.

Where the offence which is alleged to have been committed extraterritorially is one under the 2009 Act itself, or indecent assault at common law, the general provisions of s.55 should be applied to resolve any issue of temporal uncertainty.

Uncertainty as to age

Uncertainty as to the date on which a sexual offence took place may create **1.31** difficulty as to establishing the age of either or both of the parties at the relevant time. There may also be some instances where the date of the offence is established with certainty but there is for some reason uncertainty as to the date of birth of the accused or complainer. This is dealt with by way of "deeming provisions" under ss.40 and 41 of the 2009 Act, and further provisions under s.50. These provisions are considered below by reference to the circumstances in which they apply.

Where the accused is charged with an offence against an older child and there is uncertainty as to the age of the complainer

The 2009 Act addresses this difficulty by way of the first two of its four "deem- **1.32** ing provisions".[187]

Deeming provision 1 applies where A is charged with an offence against an older child, B, and there is a failure to establish beyond reasonable doubt that B had attained the age of 13 years at the relevant time. Provided it is proven beyond reasonable doubt that B had not attained the age of 16 years at the relevant time, B will be deemed to have been an older child.

Deeming provisions 2, 3 and 4 deal with the peculiarity of s.37, which creates offences of older children engaging in sexual conduct with each other.[188] Because both parties will normally be guilty of such an offence, it is possible for both A to be prosecuted and B to be prosecuted. A can therefore, uniquely in the scheme of the Act, be the complainer. Deeming provision 2 therefore provides that where B is charged with an offence against A under s.37, and there is a failure to prove that A had attained the age of 13 years at the relevant time, but it is proven that A had not attained the age of 16 years, A will be deemed to have been an older child.

---

[185] Civic Government (Scotland) Act 1982 ss.52, 52A and the Protection of Children and Prevention of Sexual Offences (Scotland) Act 2005 ss.9–12.
[186] 2009 Act s.56(3).
[187] 2009 Act ss.40, 41.
[188] See below, para.2.49.

Where the accused is charged with engaging in sexual conduct with another older child and there is uncertainty as to the age of the accused

1.33 Because the s.37 offences require the accused to have been an older child, deeming provisions 3 and 4 deal with the situation where there is doubt as to whether the accused was in fact over the age of 16 at the relevant time. Provided they are proved beyond reasonable doubt to be over the age of 13, they will be deemed to have not attained the age of 16 at the relevant time even if this is not proven beyond a reasonable doubt. They will therefore, again, be deemed to have been an older child.

The combined effect of the deeming provisions

1.34 The effect of the deeming provisions is that where it is established that the accused has committed an offence, but uncertainty as to age means it is not certain precisely what that offence is, they will always be convicted of the less serious offence.[189] That is, they will always be convicted of an offence against an older child rather than a younger child, or (where the doubt is as to whether the accused was in fact under the age of 16 at the relevant time), they will be convicted of the offence of engaging while an older child in sexual conduct with or towards an older child, rather than an offence against an older child committed by a person over the age of 16. They would, in fact, apply even where the relevant individual's status as an older child is flatly contradicted by the evidence, something which is important because a more serious offence than the one with which the accused is charged cannot be available as an alternative verdict. So, if A is charged with having sexual intercourse with an older child, it would be no defence for him to suggest or even to prove that B was in fact a younger child. Even a direct contradiction of the prosecution case is still the, "failure to prove beyond reasonable doubt" on the prosecution's part which the statute requires.[190]

Where the accused is charged with an offence against a young child and there is uncertainty as to the complainer's age

1.35 Under s.50 of the 2009 Act,[191] where A is charged with an offence against a young child, the alternative verdict of an offence against an older child is not barred by a failure to establish beyond a reasonable doubt that B had attained the age of 13 years at the relevant time.

Where the accused is charged with an offence against an older child and there is uncertainty as to the accused's age

1.36 Under s.50 of the 2009 Act,[192] if A is charged with an offence under ss.28–30 of the Act (having intercourse with an older child, engaging in penetrative sexual activity with or towards an older child and engaging in sexual activity with or towards an older child), the alternative verdicts under s.37 (older children engaging in sexual conduct with each other) are not barred by a failure to establish beyond a reasonable doubt that A had not attained the age of 16 by the relevant time.

---

[189] But cf. Brown, *Sexual Offences (Scotland) Act 2009*, p.70, who suggests that deeming provision 4 (which applies where B is charged with an offence under s.37(4)) means B could wrongly be convicted when he has done something he has a perfect right to do. This seems impossible: conviction under s.37(4) would require proof that A is under 16, and B has no right to engage in sexual activity with A while A is under that age.

[190] cf. Brown, *Sexual Offences (Scotland) Act 2009*, p.70, who suggests that this requirement could mean that the deeming provisions cannot apply where there is no sufficiency of evidence. It is difficult to see why this should be so: failures to lead a sufficiency of evidence are necessarily a subset of failures to prove beyond reasonable doubt.

[191] 2009 Act s.50(2), (3).

[192] 2009 Act s.50(2), (4).

Interaction with existing rules on special capacity and presumptions as to age

The accused's age is a special capacity and so, when libelled in the indictment **1.37** or complaint, will be held to be admitted unless timeously objected to.[193] In addition, specification of the age of A and/or B in the indictment or complaint triggers the rule in s.46(3) of the Criminal Procedure (Scotland) Act 1995,[194] which provides that where:

> "... it is alleged that the person by or in respect of whom the offence was committed was a child or was under or had attained any specified age, and he appears to the court to have been at the date of the commission of the alleged offence a child, or to have been under or to have attained the specified age, as the case may be, he shall for the purposes of this Act ... be presumed at that date to have been a child or to have been under or to have attained that age, as the case may be, unless the contrary is proved."

There are some difficulties with this provision, not least that it is not clear what "purposes of the Act" means.[195] Assuming it means a criminal prosecution brought under the provisions of the Act,[196] then its effect is that if either A or B is alleged to have been a child, or if A is alleged to have attained the age of 16 (as is necessary for certain offences under the 2009 Act), then this will be presumed until the contrary is proven. But because s.46(3) only goes so far as creating a presumption that a person was "a child", it cannot be used to set up a presumption that any person was an "older child" or a "young child". However, the deeming provisions require proof that the individual who is to be deemed as having been an older child had not attained the age of 16 years. Section 46(3) supplies that proof. It follows that if A or B is specified in a complaint or indictment as having been a child at the relevant time and no evidence whatsoever is led as to age, they will be deemed to be an older child.

Extraterritorial Jurisdiction and Sexual Offences

Pressure in the 1990s to take action against what has been described as "sex **1.38** tourism"—the sexual abuse of children by British citizens in third world countries—resulted in the UK Government passing legislation taking extraterritorial jurisdiction over first, actions in Scotland amounting to conspiracy or incitement to commit child sexual offences abroad[197] and shortly thereafter, jurisdiction over child sexual offences committed abroad by British citizens

---

[193] Criminal Procedure (Scotland) Act 1995 s.255. But cf. Brown, *Sexual Offences (Scotland) Act 2009*, p.69.

[194] Which is made applicable to relevant offences in the 2009 Act by Sch.5 para.8 of the latter statute.

[195] There might also be some doubt as to whether it should be read as imposing an evidential or a legal burden on the accused. A reverse burden in respect of the accused's own age is relatively easy to justify—this is something within his own knowledge which he should be able to prove with relative ease—but it is less clear why the accused should bear a legal burden in respect of the complainer's age. Accordingly, s.46(3) of the 1995 Act might be read as imposing a legal burden on the accused in respect of his or her own age, but an evidential burden only in respect of the complainer's age. On the general issue of reverse burdens, see further Ian Dennis, "Reverse Onuses and the Presumption of Innocence: In Search of Principle" [2005] Crim. L.R. 901.

[196] This, however, is problematic. The text, "for the purposes of this Act" in s.46(3) is followed immediately by, "or the Children and Young Persons (Scotland) Act 1937 or Part I of the Criminal Law (Consolidation) (Scotland) Act 1995". If the reading of the provision in the text were correct, this additional text would be unnecessary. The 2009 Act does not, as would have been desirable, amend the text of s.46(3) itself to include a reference to the 2009 Act. Conversely, the argument in favour of the reading offered in the text is that if, "for the purposes of this Act" is narrowly interpreted, the amendment of paras 3 and 4 of the Schedule to the 1995 Act (which specifies which offences s.46(3) applies to) by Sch.5 para.8 of the 2009 Act would be largely redundant.

[197] Sexual Offences (Conspiracy and Incitement) Act 1996 s.6, inserting s.16A into the Criminal Law (Consolidation) (Scotland) Act 1995.

or residents.[198] Although motivated by activities in third world countries, these provisions were not limited in their extraterritorial ambit, and the equivalent English provisions have resulted in prosecutions in respect of activities occurring in countries such as Barbados,[199] Denmark[200] and France.[201] The relevant provisions have been repeated, with some modification, in the 2009 Act.

Offences committed outside the United Kingdom

1.39 This matter is now dealt with by s.55 of the 2009 Act, which applies to the offences listed in Pt 2 of Sch.4 to the Act (the "listed offences"). The list of offences is similar in nature to that found under earlier legislation, except that it is now concerned with children under the age of 18 rather than 16.[202]

Part 2 of Sch.4 lists those offences specifically concerned with child victims,[203] along with general offences where committed against a person under the age of 18.[204] A number of other statutory offences are listed.[205] Two general provisions at the end of Pt 2 extend the list's ambit to conspiracy or incitement to commit any of the listed offences.[206] Surprisingly, the list does not extend to attempts to commit the listed offences,[207] even though the provisions on resolution of temporal uncertainty in respect of extraterritorial offending do,[208] something which seems to make no sense if the provisions which confer extraterritorial jurisdiction do not encompass attempts. The drafting may rest on the theory that the statutory rule which states that any attempt to commit an offence is itself an offence[209] means that the Scottish courts necessarily have jurisdiction over an attempt where they would have jurisdiction over a completed crime, but it seems unsatisfactory for the legal position to rest on this untested assumption.

---

[198] Sex Offenders Act 1997 s.8, inserting s.16B into the Criminal Law (Consolidation) (Scotland) Act 1995. On the 1996 and 1997 Acts, see generally Peter Alldridge, "The Sexual Offences (Conspiracy and Incitement) Act 1996" [1997] Crim. L.R. 30; Peter Alldridge, "Sex Offenders Act 1997—Territoriality Provisions" [1997] Crim. L.R. 655; Michael Hirst, *Jurisdiction and the Ambit of the Criminal Law* (Oxford: Oxford University Press, 2003), pp.139–142, 268–271.

[199] *R. v R (Peter)* [2001] 1 W.L.R. 1314, where the conviction was quashed on the basis that the acts in question had taken place before the legislation came into force.

[200] *R. v Holderness (Stephen)* [2004] EWCA Crim 3177.

[201] See below, fn.207.

[202] This seems to be in order to comply with the 2007 Council of Europe Convention on the Protection of Children Against Sexual Exploitation and Sexual Abuse, which the United Kingdom signed in 2008 but has not yet ratified. Article 3 of the Convention defines "child" as, "any person under the age of 18 years".

[203] That is, offences under Pt 4 and s.42 (sexual abuse of trust) of the 2009 Act.

[204] That is, offences under Pt 1 and s.46 (sexual abuse of trust of a mentally disordered person) of the 2009 Act, and the common law offence of indecent assault.

[205] Civic Government (Scotland) Act 1982 ss.52, 52A and the Protection of Children and Prevention of Sexual Offences (Scotland) Act 2005 ss.9–12.

[206] 2009 Act Sch.4 Pt 2 para.17. Liability under s.293(2) of the Criminal Procedure (Scotland) Act 1995 (statutory offences: art and part and aiding and abetting) is also included: para.18. There is no reference to art and part liability, presumably on the basis that this is unnecessary given that an actor who is guilty art and part is guilty of the full offence, but cf. s.56(4)(d).

[207] Unlike the equivalent provisions in English law: Sexual Offences Act 2003 Sch.2 para.3. This discrepancy is also present in the original legislation which created this form of extraterritorial jurisdiction for both Scots and English law: see Sex Offenders Act 1997 s.8, Sch.2 para.3. Because both the Scottish and English legislation applies to "UK nationals", an extraterritorial attempt by a UK national from Scotland to commit a sexual offence against a child could be prosecuted in England, even if the accused had never been to England. In September 2009, a Scottish defendant pled guilty in London to inter alia the attempted rape of a nine-year-old boy while on a trip to France: see "Teacher admits trying to rape boy", *BBC News Online*, September 15, 2009. However, it is unlikely that jurisdiction over attempts was a factor in determining where the prosecution took place. The complaint had been made to the Metropolitan Police in London, and under Scots law as it stood at the time any Scottish prosecution would (depending on the exact facts of the case) probably have been for indecent assault rather than an attempted crime.

[208] 2009 Act s.56(4)(a).

[209] Criminal Procedure (Scotland) Act 1995 s.294.

A distinction is drawn between UK nationals and UK residents. Where a UK national does an act abroad which would have constituted a listed offence if done in Scotland, then they are regarded as having committed that offence.[210] It matters not whether their act amounted to an offence under the law of that country. United Kingdom nationals effectively carry the UK's rules on the age of consent with them when they travel abroad: a UK national who engages in sexual activity with a 15-year-old abroad commits a criminal offence even if the age of consent in that country is 15 or less.[211] For UK residents, however, there is an additional requirement: the act must have constituted an offence under the law in force in the country where they committed the act. This condition will be deemed to be satisfied unless the accused timeously serves a notice on the prosecutor disputing the point.[212] The question of whether the condition is satisfied is for the judge alone and not any jury which may be empanelled.[213]

Section 55 can be applied either whether the accused was a UK national or UK resident at the time the relevant conduct took place or where he has subsequently acquired that status.[214] Although the concept of a "UK national" is defined by reference to existing legal concepts,[215] "UK resident" is not: it has been suggested that it may simply mean voluntary physical presence as an inhabitant.[216]

Incitement to commit certain sexual acts outside the United Kingdom

This matter is dealt with by s.54 of the 2009 Act, and concerns a smaller **1.40** number of listed offences (a subset of those to which s.55 applies).[217] Section 54 applies where a person does an act in Scotland which would amount to incitement to commit one of these offences but for the fact that the conduct is intended to occur outside the United Kingdom. In such a case, they can be convicted of incitement to commit the listed offence, subject only to the caveat that if they are not a UK national they can be convicted only if the law in force in the relevant country[218] would also render the intended conduct an offence.[219]

Although s.55 itself applies to incitement to commit acts abroad, the provision applies only where a UK national, "does an act in a country outside the United Kingdom".[220] It will therefore be necessary to rely on s.54 rather than s.55 where the act amounting to incitement takes place in Scotland itself. Section 54 is also capable of application to individuals who are neither UK nationals nor UK residents but who, while in Scotland, incite someone to commit a listed sexual offence abroad. Incitement by means of a mes-

---

[210] 2009 Act s.55(1).

[211] Card, Gillespie and Hirst, *Sexual Offences*, para.2.95.

[212] 2009 Act s.55(4), and see Act of Adjournal (Criminal Procedure Rules) 1996 (SI 1996/513) r.27.5. The court may dispense with the requirement for prior service with a notice: s.55(5).

[213] 2009 Act s.55(6).

[214] 2009 Act ss.54(8), 55(8).

[215] See 2009 Act ss.54(8), 55(8). The definition of UK national is broader than the British citizens to which the earlier Scottish provisions applied, now covering, in addition to British citizens, British overseas territories citizens, British nationals (overseas), British overseas citizens, British subjects and British protected persons. This duplicates changes made to English law by s.72 of the Criminal Justice and Immigration Act 2008.

[216] Brown, *Sexual Offences (Scotland) Act 2009*, p.86, citing *Inland Revenue Commissioners v Duchess of Portland* [1982] S.T.C. 149.

[217] They are offences under the 2009 Act Pt 1 (where against a person under the age of 18); Pt 4, s.42 (sexual abuse of trust), and s.46 (sexual abuse of trust of a mentally disordered person, where that person is under the age of 18), and indecent assault of a person under the age of 18.

[218] That is, "the country where the whole or any part of" the relevant conduct was intended to take place: 2009 Act s.54(2).

[219] Provisions for proof of this issue, which are identical to those applicable in respect of s.55 (above, para.1.39) are set out in the 2009 Act s.54(2)–(6).

[220] 2009 Act s.55(1).

sage is to be treated as done in Scotland if the message is sent or received in Scotland.[221]

ALTERNATIVE VERDICTS

1.41 Section 50 and Sch.3 of the Act make provision for alternative verdicts, specifying alternative offences in respect of most of the offences created by the 2009 Act. Where the accused is charged with an offence under the 2009 Act and that offence is not made out, but the jury (in solemn procedure) or judge (in summary procedure) is satisfied that the accused committed one of the specified alternative offences, the accused may be acquitted of the charge but convicted of the alternative offence.

Most of the specified alternative offences are offences under the 2009 Act itself, but some are offences at common law. It is not clear how this interacts with Sch.3 para.14 of the Criminal Procedure (Scotland) Act 1995, which provides as follows:

> "Where—
>   (a)   any act alleged in an indictment or complaint as contrary to any enactment is also criminal at common law; or
>   (b)   where the facts proved under the indictment or complaint do not amount to a contravention of the enactment, but do amount to an offence at common law,
> it shall be lawful to convict of the common law offence."

The specific alternative verdict scheme created by the 2009 Act, encompassing common law offences, may mean that the general Sch.3 para.14 rule is displaced. That would be no bad thing, as this rule is so broad as potentially to deprive the accused of fair notice of the offences of which he could be convicted.[222] Offences not specified in Sch.3 of the 2009 Act can nonetheless be charged in the alternative where appropriate.

---

[221] 2009 Act s.55(7). Consequently, if A, in country X, emails B inviting B to commit a child sex offence in country X, and B receives the email in Scotland, A commits an offence in Scotland even if he has never been there. This is so even if A and B are both nationals of country X but B receives the email while on holiday.

[222] See *Report*, para 7.20, although the view expressed there about the European Convention on Human Rights may go too far: see Brown, *Sexual Offences (Scotland) Act 2009*, p.79.

CHAPTER 2

THE SPECIAL PART

To assist the reader in using this chapter, the following table lists the offences **2.01** created by the 2009 Act along with the paragraph number where the discussion of that offence begins.

Section	Offence name	Para.
1	Rape	2.02
2	Sexual assault by penetration	2.06
3	Sexual assault	2.10
4	Sexual coercion	2.15
5	Coercing a person into being present during a sexual activity	2.19
6	Coercing a person into looking at a sexual image	2.23
7(1)	Communicating indecently	2.27
7(2)	Causing a person to see or hear an indecent communication	2.30
8	Sexual exposure	2.34
9	Voyeurism	2.38
11	Administering a substance for sexual purposes	2.43
18	Rape of a young child	2.03
19	Sexual assault on a young child by penetration	2.07
20	Sexual assault on a young child	2.11
21	Causing a young child to participate in a sexual activity	2.17
22	Causing a young child to be present during a sexual activity	2.21
23	Causing a young child to look at a sexual image	2.25
24(1)	Communicating indecently with a young child	2.29
24(2)	Causing a young child to see or hear an indecent communication	2.31
25	Sexual exposure to a young child	2.36
26	Voyeurism towards a young child	2.41
28	Having intercourse with an older child	2.45
29	Engaging in penetrative sexual activity with or towards an older child	2.46
30	Engaging in sexual activity with or towards an older child	2.47
31	Causing an older child to participate in a sexual activity	2.16
32	Causing an older child to be present during a sexual activity	2.20
33	Causing an older child to look at a sexual image	2.24
34(1)	Communicating indecently with an older child	2.29
34(2)	Causing an older child to see or hear an indecent communication	2.31
35	Sexual exposure to an older child	2.35
36	Voyeurism towards an older child	2.40
37(1)	Engaging while an older child in sexual conduct with or towards another older child	2.49
37(4)	Engaging while an older child in consensual sexual conduct with or towards another older child	2.49
42	Sexual abuse of trust	2.52
43	Sexual abuse of trust of a mentally disordered person	2.55

RAPE

2.02 At common law, the actus reus of rape was understood until 2002 as the carnal knowledge of a female by a male person obtained by overcoming her will.[1] Despite this well-understood formulation (which meant that having sexual intercourse with a sleeping woman was not rape, but the crime of "clandestine injury"),[2] the offence of rape was perhaps commonly—if wrongly—understood as being based on the absence of consent rather than the overcoming of the will.[3] The law formally changed in *Lord Advocate's Reference (No.1 of 2001)*,[4] where the appeal court held—overruling prior authority—that the actus reus of rape should be understood as a man having sexual intercourse with a woman without her consent. Sexual intercourse, for these purposes, was restricted to penile-vaginal penetration.[5]

The mens rea of rape was knowledge that the woman was not consenting or recklessness as to whether she was consenting.[6] Recklessness in this context was understood subjectively, meaning that if A had an honest belief that B was consenting, he lacked the mens rea of rape regardless of whether that belief was reasonable or unreasonable.[7]

The Scottish Law Commission recommended that while rape should continue to be defined in relation to the absence of consent and restricted to penile penetration (a "specific wrong" distinct from other penetrative assaults), it should encompass anal and oral penetration in addition to vaginal penetration.[8] Such a change means that men, as well as women, can be the victims of rape.[9] The

---

[1]   Gordon, *Criminal Law*, para.33.01; Hume, i, 301–303; Alison, *Principles*, p.209; Burnett, *Criminal Law*, p.109; Macdonald, *Criminal Law*, p.119. The writers up to and including Macdonald emphasised that the will had to be "forcibly" overcome; Gordon downplays this requirement but seems to limit "overcoming the will" to cases of force, drugging and possibly certain types of fraud: paras 33.05–33.07. The rule that a husband could not in law rape his wife, if it was ever part of Scots law, was dispensed with by *S v HM Advocate*, 1989 S.L.T. 469.

[2]   *Charles Sweenie* (1858) 3 Irv. 109. A majority of the judges in the earlier case of *William Fraser* (1847) Ark. 280 had thought that the "overcoming of the will"—as opposed to a mere absence of consent—was not essential to the crime. That point was, however, obscured by the specific issue which the *Fraser* court had to decide (whether a man who had sexual intercourse with a woman by impersonating her husband committed rape), and therefore did not prevent the *Sweenie* court from taking the approach it did.

[3]   So in *McDade (Richard Carlyle) v HM Advocate*, 1998 S.L.T. 68, the appellant was charged with rape but instead convicted of incest. The trial judge concluded that the jury's verdict meant only that force had not been used to overcome the complainer's will, and sentenced on the basis that she had nonetheless not consented to the intercourse. On appeal, it was held that the trial judge had erred, with Lord Sutherland asserting at 69 that: "If it is alleged that the woman concerned did not consent, the proper approach is to charge rape ... The jury have however negatived that aspect ...". It is difficult to see how the jury could be regarded as having done any such thing given the basis on which they had been charged, but the appeal court's approach is indicative of the extent to which rape had come to be regarded as a crime based on the absence of consent rather than the overcoming of the will, despite the contrary state of the authorities at the time. See also Victor Tadros, "No Consent: A Historical Critique of the Actus Reus of Rape" (1999) 3 Edin. L.R. 317, 317, 318.

[4]   *Lord Advocate's Reference (No.1 of 2001)*, 2002 S.L.T. 466. See James Chalmers, "How (Not) To Reform the Law of Rape" (2002) 6 Edin. L.R. 388.

[5]   See Gordon, *Criminal Law*, para.33.02.

[6]   *Lord Advocate's Reference (No 1 of 2001)*, 2002 S.L.T. 466, per the Lord Justice-General (Cullen) at [44].

[7]   *Jamieson (Brian) v HM Advocate*, 1994 J.C. 88. This followed the approach taken by the House of Lords in the leading (and highly controversial) English case of *DPP v Morgan (William Anthony)* [1976] A.C. 182. The rule in *Morgan* was effectively overruled by the Sexual Offences Act 2003, and the 2009 Act mirrors this development for Scotland.

[8]   *Report*, paras 3.23–3.28. For discussion of the proposals outlined by the Commission in its *Discussion Paper*, and suggestions for alternative models for reform, see Pamela R. Ferguson and Fiona E. Raitt, "Reforming the Scots Law of Rape: Redefining the Offence" (2006) 10 Edin. L.R. 185.

[9]   This lags well behind parallel developments in English law, where "male rape" has been recognised since s.142 of the Criminal Justice and Public Order Act 1994.

Commission also recommended that—as with other sexual offences—the mens rea should be the absence of a reasonable belief in B's consent, in addition to A having intended to penetrate B or being reckless as to whether there was penetration. (This is the model adopted throughout the 2009 Act in relation to mens rea and consent.) Accordingly, rape is defined by s.1 of the Act as follows[10]:

> "(1) If a person ('A'), with A's penis—
>   (a)   without another person ('B') consenting, and
>   (b)   without any reasonable belief that B consents,
> penetrates to any extent, either intending to do so or reckless as to whether there is penetration, the vagina, anus or mouth of B then A commits an offence, to be known as the offence of rape.
>   (2) For the purposes of this section, penetration is a continuing act from entry until withdrawal of the penis; but this subsection is subject to subsection (3).
>   (3) In a case where penetration is initially consented to but at some point of time the consent is withdrawn, subsection (2) is to be construed as if the reference in it to a continuing act from entry were a reference to a continuing act from that point of time.
>   (4) In this Act—
>   "penis" includes a surgically constructed penis if it forms part of A, having been created in the course of surgical treatment, and
>   "vagina" includes—
>   (a)   the vulva, and
>   (b)   a surgically constructed vagina (together with any surgically constructed vulva), if it forms part of B, having been created in the course of such treatment."

This offence carries a maximum penalty, on conviction on indictment, of life imprisonment, which may be accompanied by a fine.[11] Four offences are specified as possible alternative verdicts.[12] The offence may be committed outwith the United Kingdom where A is a UK national or resident and B is under the age of 18.[13]

Modified offence in respect of young children

An offence of rape of a young child is created by s.18 of the 2009 Act. This **2.03** offence is committed where:

> "... a person ('A'), with A's penis, penetrates to any extent, either intending to do so or reckless as to whether there is penetration, the vagina, anus or mouth of a child ('B') who has not attained the age of 13 years".

Consent is irrelevant, and it is no defence that A believed B had attained the age of 13 years.[14]

This offence carries a maximum penalty, on conviction on indictment, of life imprisonment, which may be accompanied by a fine.[15] Six offences are

---

[10]   This is identical to s.1 of the Commission's draft Bill (*Report*, p.137), save that, "surgically constructed" in subs.(4) replaces the terminology of "artificial" used in the Commission's draft.

[11]   2009 Act Sch.2. The court may not impose a penalty of a fine alone: see s.48. This provision is the result of concerns which were raised as the Bill went through Parliament about the possibility of a fine alone being imposed as a penalty for rape: see Brown, *Sexual Offences (Scotland) Act 2009*, p.77.

[12]   2009 Act Sch.3. These are: sexual assault by penetration (s.2); sexual assault (s.3); having intercourse with an older child (s.28); and assault at common law.

[13]   2009 Act s.55, Sch.4 Pt 2. On extraterritorial jurisdiction, see above, para.1.39.

[14]   2009 Act s.27. See above, para.1.20.

[15]   2009 Act Sch.2. The court may not impose a penalty of a fine alone: see s.48 and above, fn.11

specified as possible alternative verdicts.[16] The offence may be committed out-with the United Kingdom where A is a UK national or resident.[17]

The position of older children

2.04 There is no direct equivalent of this offence in respect of older children. Where A has consensual sexual intercourse with an older child (B), this is not regarded as rape despite B's inability to give a legally valid consent. Instead, the offence of having intercourse with an older child (s.28) applies.[18] Non-consensual intercourse with an older child should simply be prosecuted as rape under s.1 of the Act.

The elements of the offence

2.05 The core elements of the offence are the absence of consent on B's part and the corresponding absence of a reasonable belief in consent on the part of A. These are both common to the scheme of the Act as a whole and are discussed earlier in this volume.[19] On other aspects of the offence, it should be noted that while penile penetration is required, the offence is drafted in gender-neutral terms: it can be committed by any person and "penis" includes a surgically constructed penis. This avoids any difficult questions which might otherwise arise as the result of gender reassignment.

SEXUAL ASSAULT BY PENETRATION

2.06 The Scottish Law Commission did not recommend a separate offence of sexual assault by penetration, concluding instead that this should be a recognised mode of committing the offence of sexual assault. However, in response to evidence taken by the Justice Committee in its scrutiny of the Bill and the Committee's recommendations,[20] Government amendments were lodged to create such an offence. Section 2 of the 2009 Act defines the offence of sexual assault by penetration in the following terms:

> "(1) If a person ('A'), with any part of A's body or anything else —
>> (a)   without another person ('B') consenting, and
>> (b)   without any reasonable belief that B consents,
> penetrates sexually to any extent, either intending to do so or reckless as to whether there is penetration, the vagina or anus of B then A commits an offence, to be known as the offence of sexual assault by penetration.
>
>> (2) For the purposes of this section, penetration is a continuing act from entry to withdrawal of whatever is intruded; but this subsection is subject to subsection (3).
>
>> (3) In a case where penetration is initially consented to but at some point of time the consent is withdrawn, subsection (2) is to be construed as if the reference in it to a continuing act from entry were a reference to a continuing act from that point of time.
>
>> (4) Without prejudice to the generality of subsection (1), the reference in that subsection to penetration with any part of A's body is to be construed as including a reference to penetration with A's penis."

---

[16]   2009 Act Sch.3. These are: sexual assault on a young child by penetration (s.19); sexual assault on a young child (s.20); having intercourse with an older child (s.28); engaging in penetrative sexual activity with or towards an older child (s.29); engaging in sexual activity with or towards an older child (s.30); engaging while an older child in sexual conduct with or towards another older child (s.37(1)); and assault at common law.

[17]   2009 Act s.55, Sch.4 Pt 2. On extraterritorial jurisdiction, see above, para.1.39.

[18]   See below, para.2.45. If A is also an older child, he will instead have committed an offence under s.37 (older children engaging in sexual conduct with each other). See below, para.2.49.

[19]   See above, paras 1.03 et seq. (consent) and 1.23 (reasonable belief in consent).

[20]   See Justice Committee, *Stage 1 Report on the Sexual Offences (Scotland) Bill, 1st Report* (Scottish Parliament, 2009), SP Paper 194 (Session 3), paras 82–97.

This offence carries a maximum penalty, on conviction on indictment, of life imprisonment, which may be accompanied by a fine.[21] Four offences are specified as possible alternative verdicts.[22] The offence may be committed outwith the United Kingdom where A is a UK national or resident and B is under the age of 18.[23]

Modified offence in respect of young children

An offence of sexual assault of a young child by penetration is created by s.19 **2.07** of the 2009 Act. The offence is defined in the same terms as s.2, save that B must not have attained the age of 13 years and consent is irrelevant. It is no defence that A believed B had attained the age of 13 years.[24]

This offence carries a maximum penalty, on conviction on indictment, of life imprisonment, which may be accompanied by a fine.[25] Six offences are specified as possible alternative verdicts.[26] The offence may be committed outwith the United Kingdom where A is a UK national or resident.[27]

The position of older children

There is no direct equivalent of this offence in respect of older children. Where **2.08** A has consensual sexual intercourse with an older child (B), this is not regarded as rape despite B's inability to give a legally valid consent. Instead, the offence of engaging in penetrative sexual activity with or towards an older child (s.29) applies.[28] Non-consensual penetration of an older child should simply be prosecuted under s.2 of the Act.

The elements of the offence

The core elements of the offence, beyond penetration, are the absence of con- **2.09** sent on B's part and the corresponding absence of a reasonable belief in consent on the part of A. These are both common to the scheme of the Act as a whole and are discussed earlier in this volume.[29] It should be noted that penile penetration falls within the ambit of the offence. While any such case would be rape (assuming the other elements of the offence could be proven), this avoids a case where there is uncertainty as to whether penetration was penile or non-penile[30] falling between two stools and being prosecutable as neither rape nor sexual assault by penetration.

---

[21] 2009 Act Sch.2. The court may not impose a penalty of a fine alone: see s.48 and above, fn.11.

[22] 2009 Act Sch.3. These are: sexual assault (s.3); engaging in penetrative sexual activity with or towards an older child (s.29); engaging in sexual activity with or towards an older child (s.30); and assault at common law.

[23] 2009 Act s.55, Sch.4 Pt 2. On extraterritorial jurisdiction, see above, para.1.39.

[24] 2009 Act s.27. See above, para.1.20.

[25] 2009 Act Sch.2. The court may not impose a penalty of a fine alone: see s.48 and above, fn.11.

[26] 2009 Act Sch.3. These are: sexual assault on a young child (s.20); engaging in penetrative sexual activity with or towards an older child (s.30); engaging in sexual activity with or towards an older child (s.30); and assault at common law.

[27] 2009 Act s.55, Sch.4 Pt 2. On extraterritorial jurisdiction, see above, para.1.39.

[28] See below, para.2.46. If A is also an older child, he will instead have committed an offence under s.37 (older children engaging in sexual conduct with each other). See below, para.2.49.

[29] See above, paras 1.03–1.14 and 1.23.

[30] See, e.g. *Garvock v HM Advocate*, 1991 S.C.C.R. 593.

SEXUAL ASSAULT

2.10 The offence of sexual assault is defined by s.3 of the 2009 Act in the following
terms[31]:

> "(1) If a person ('A')—
>
> (a)   without another person ('B') consenting, and
> (b)   without any reasonable belief that B consents,
> does any of the things mentioned in subsection (2), then A commits an
> offence, to be known as the offence of sexual assault.
> (2) Those things are, that A—
> (a)   penetrates sexually, by any means and to any extent, either
>   intending to do so or reckless as to whether there is penetration,
>   the vagina, anus or mouth of B,
> (b)   intentionally or recklessly touches B sexually,
> (c)   engages in any other form of sexual activity in which A,
>   intentionally or recklessly, has physical contact (whether bodily
>   contact or contact by means of an implement and whether or not
>   through clothing) with B,
> (d)   intentionally or recklessly ejaculates semen onto B,
> (e)   intentionally or recklessly emits urine or saliva onto B sexually.
> (3) For the purposes of paragraph (a) of subsection (2), penetration is
> a continuing act from entry until withdrawal of whatever is intruded; but
> this subsection is subject to subsection (4).
> (4) In a case where penetration is initially consented to but at some
> point of time the consent is withdrawn, subsection (3) is to be construed
> as if the reference in it to a continuing act from entry were a reference to
> a continuing act from that point of time.
> (5) Without prejudice to the generality of paragraph (a) of subsection
> (2), the reference in the paragraph to penetration by any means is to be
> construed as including a reference to penetration with A's penis."

The offence carries a maximum penalty, on summary conviction, of 12 months'
imprisonment and/or a fine not exceeding the statutory maximum and, on conviction on indictment, of life imprisonment and/or a fine.[32] Two offences are
specified as possible alternative verdicts.[33] The offence may be committed outwith the United Kingdom where A is a UK national or resident and B is under
the age of 18.[34]

Modified offence in respect of young children

2.11 An offence of sexual assault of a young child is created by s.20 of the 2009
Act. The offence is defined in the same terms as s.3, save that B must not have
attained the age of 13 years and consent is irrelevant. It is no defence that A
believed B had attained the age of 13 years.[35]

   This offence carries a maximum penalty, on summary conviction, of 12
months' imprisonment and/or a fine not exceeding the statutory maximum
and, on conviction on indictment, of life imprisonment and/or a fine.[36] Four

---

[31]   This provision is broadly similar to s.2 of the Scottish Law Commission's draft Bill (*Report*,
pp.138, 139), save for the addition of, "intentionally or recklessly emit[ting] urine or saliva onto B
sexually" as a "thing" which can constitute the offence. This was included by amendment during
the Bill's progress through Parliament.
[32]   2009 Act Sch.2.
[33]   2009 Act Sch.3. These are: engaging in sexual activity with or towards an older child (s.30)
and assault at common law.
[34]   2009 Act s.55, Sch.4 Pt 2. On extraterritorial jurisdiction, see above, para.1.39.
[35]   2009 Act s.27. See above, para.1.20.
[36]   2009 Act Sch.2.

offences are specified as possible alternative verdicts.[37] The offence may be committed outwith the United Kingdom where A is a UK national or resident.[38]

The position of older children

There is no direct equivalent of this offence in respect of older children. Where **2.12** A engages in consensual sexual activity with an older child (B), the offence of engaging in sexual activity with or towards an older child (s.30) applies.[39]

Relationship with indecent assault at common law

The common law offence of indecent assault is not, strictly speaking, an of- **2.13** fence in itself, but, "simply an assault accompanied by circumstances of indecency".[40] The Scottish Law Commission recommended that, notwithstanding the creation of a statutory offence of sexual assault, the common law position be left unaltered, on the basis that there might, "be other ways in which a person can be subject to a sexual attack".[41] There is something odd about this line of reasoning, which seems to imply an admission that the definition of "sexual assault" proposed by the Commission was somehow inadequate. The example given by the Commission was that where A urinated on B, this might be an indecent assault depending on the facts and circumstances, but that particular example was met by the Bill being amended on its passage through Parliament to encompass cases where A, "emits urine or saliva onto B sexually".[42]

Although indecent assault technically remains a competent charge, this is subject to s.52(b) of the 2009 Act, which provides that, "in so far as the provisions of this Act regulate any conduct they replace any rule of law regulating that conduct". Its practical use will therefore be very limited.[43]

The elements of the offence

The core elements of the offence are the absence of consent on B's part and **2.14** the corresponding absence of a reasonable belief in consent on the part of A. These are both common to the scheme of the Act as a whole and are discussed earlier in this volume.[44] Penetration, penile or otherwise, falls within the ambit of the offence. While this means that conduct constituting either the offence of rape or sexual assault by penetration also falls within the ambit of the offence of sexual assault, this avoids any cases where there is uncertainty as to the presence of penetration being prosecutable as neither rape nor sexual assault by penetration, nor sexual assault.

SEXUAL COERCION AND CAUSING CHILDREN TO PARTICIPATE IN SEXUAL ACTIVITY

The Scottish Law Commission considered that an offence was necessary to **2.15** cover the situation where A compels B to engage in sexual activity which did not necessarily involve contact with A, noting that it was not clear how this

---

[37] 2009 Act Sch.3. These are: engaging in sexual activity with or towards an older child (s.29); engaging while an older child in sexual conduct with or towards another older child (s.37(1)); engaging while an older child in consensual sexual conduct with another older child (s.37(4)); and assault at common law.

[38] 2009 Act s.55, Sch.4 Pt 2. On extraterritorial jurisdiction, see above, para.1.39.

[39] See below, para.2.47. If A is also an older child, he cannot commit this offence but may have committed an offence under s.37 (older children engaging in sexual conduct with each other). See below, para.2.49.

[40] Gordon, *Criminal Law*, para.29.24.

[41] *Report*, para.3.46.

[42] 2009 Act ss.3(2)(e), 20(2)(e).

[43] However, there might be cases in which an assault which was not in its entirety a sexual assault was in part aggravated by circumstances of indecency: the preservation of the common law rule means that these circumstances could competently be libelled in the indictment or complaint.

[44] See above, paras 1.03–1.14 and 1.23.

was dealt with under the then-existing law.[45] The offence of sexual coercion is defined in the following terms by s.4 of the 2009 Act[46]:

> "If a person ('A')—
>   (a)   without another person ('B') consenting to participate in a sexual activity, and
>   (b)   without any reasonable belief that B consents to participating in that activity,
> intentionally causes B to participate in that activity, then A commits an offence, to be known as the offence of sexual coercion."

The offence carries a maximum penalty, on summary conviction, of 12 months' imprisonment and/or a fine not exceeding the statutory maximum and, on conviction on indictment, of life imprisonment and/or a fine.[47] Six offences are specified as possible alternative verdicts.[48] The offence may be committed outwith the United Kingdom where A is a UK national or resident and B is under the age of 18.[49]

There are modified versions of this offence in respect of both older and young children (ss.31 and 21 respectively, which are discussed immediately below). Both of these offences, however, are based simply on causing the child to participate in sexual activity: there is no issue of consent. It follows that where it is alleged that an older child has been coerced into non-consensual sexual activity, s.4 is the appropriate charge, with s.31 available as an alternative verdict. It would not be appropriate for the Crown to proceed under s.31—which carries a lower maximum sentence than the s.4 offence—and then move for sentence on the basis that the activity had been non-consensual.[50] By contrast, because younger children lack any capacity to consent,[51] causing a younger child to participate in sexual activity should result in a charge under s.21 without any inquiry into any issue of "consent".

Modified offence in respect of older children

2.16 An offence of, "causing an older child to participate in a sexual activity" is created by s.31 of the 2009 Act.[52] This offence is committed if A has attained the age of 16, B is an older child and A intentionally causes B to participate in a sexual activity. Consent (or its absence) is irrelevant to this offence. The proximity of age defence under s.39 (that is, that the difference between A's age and B's age did not exceed two years) is available,[53] and the general defence of reasonable mistake as to age applies.[54]

This offence carries a maximum penalty, on summary conviction, of 12

---

[45]   *Report*, paras 3.48–3.51. At common law, if B's conduct was criminal (notwithstanding any defence of coercion open to B), or involved the commission of a crime by a third party, A might be guilty of that crime on an art and part basis: see Gordon, *Criminal Law*, para.5.03, but there is a lack of relevant Scottish authority.

[46]   2009 Act s.4 is in identical terms to s.3(1) of the Commission's draft Bill: *Report*, pp.139, 140.

[47]   2009 Act Sch.2.

[48]   2009 Act Sch.3. These are: coercing a person into being present during a sexual activity (s.5); coercing a person into looking at a sexual image (s.6); communicating indecently (s.7(1)); causing a person to see or hear an indecent communication (s.7(2)); causing an older child to participate in a sexual activity (s.31); or assault at common law.

[49]   2009 Act s.55, Sch.4 Pt 2. On extraterritorial jurisdiction, see above, para.1.39.

[50]   See *McDade v HM Advocate*, 1998 S.L.T. 68, where a similar point is made about the relationship between the offences of incest and rape.

[51]   See *Report*, paras 4.26–4.31.

[52]   See *Report*, para.4.51.

[53]   2009 Act s.39(3). See above, para.1.18.

[54]   On this defence, see above, para.1.21.

months' imprisonment and/or a fine not exceeding the statutory maximum and, on conviction on indictment, of 10 years' imprisonment and/or a fine.[55] Four offences are specified as possible alternative verdicts.[56] The offence may be committed outwith the United Kingdom where A is a UK national or resident.[57]

Modified offence in respect of young children

An offence of, "causing a young child to participate in a sexual activity" is cre- **2.17** ated by s.21 of the 2009 Act.[58] This offence is committed if B is a young child and A intentionally causes B to participate in a sexual activity. It is no defence that A believed B had attained the age of 13 years.[59]

This offence carries a maximum penalty, on summary conviction, of 12 months' imprisonment and/or a fine not exceeding the statutory maximum and, on conviction on indictment, of life imprisonment and/or a fine.[60] Eleven offences are specified as possible alternative verdicts.[61] The offence may be committed outwith the United Kingdom where A is a UK national or resident.[62]

The elements of the coercion and causation offences

The elements of these offences are mostly ones which are common to the **2.18** scheme of the 2009 Act as a whole.[63] The one exception is the element of "causing" B to participate in the activity, which is not defined.[64] The classical view of this issue would be to say that it is insufficient that B's behaviour would not have occurred but for A's. Beyond that, it must additionally be shown that B's conduct is "not wholly voluntary", that is, "the means used amount to coercion, deceit, or the exercise of authority; but not ... mere persuasion".[65] The Scottish courts, however, have declined to adopt any such clear statement, saying simply that a voluntary action, "will not necessarily break the chain of causation".[66] That approach, regrettably, provides no guidance as to *when* the causal chain will be broken.

In the context of the ss.4 and 21 offences, the fact that B's participation must be non-consensual (under s.4) or is necessarily non-consensual (under s.21), and that A should have intended it, means that it should be sufficient to limit

---

[55] 2009 Act Sch.2.

[56] 2009 Act Sch.3. These are: causing an older child to be present during a sexual activity (s.32); causing an older child to look at a sexual image (s.33); communicating indecently with an older child (s.34(1)); and causing an older child to see or hear an indecent communication (s.34(2)).

[57] 2009 Act s.55, Sch.4 Pt 2. On extraterritorial jurisdiction, see above, para.1.39.

[58] See *Report*, paras 4.21–4.31.

[59] 2009 Act s.27. See above, para.1.20.

[60] 2009 Act Sch.2.

[61] 2009 Act Sch.3. These are: causing a young child to be present during a sexual activity (s.22); causing a young child to look at a sexual image (s.23); communicating indecently with a young child (s.24(1)); causing a young child to see or hear an indecent communication (s.24(2)); causing an older child to participate in a sexual activity (s.31); causing an older child to be present during a sexual activity (s.32); causing an older child to look at a sexual image (s.33); communicating indecently with an older child (s.34(1)); causing an older child to see or hear an indecent communication (s.34(2)); and assault at common law.

[62] 2009 Act s.55, Sch.4 Pt 2. On extraterritorial jurisdiction, see above, para.1.39.

[63] See above, paras 1.01–1.14 and 1.23.

[64] The Commission said merely that, "cause is not defined but we would expect that it would be understood in the sense of proximate cause. For example, it would not be coerced sexual activity where B entered into prostitution as a result of the failure of A (her husband) to aliment her" (*Report*, para.3.53). But if A had intended (as the offence requires) that his failure have this result, why not?

[65] Herbert L.A. Hart and Tony Honoré, *Causation in the Law*, 2nd edn (Oxford: Clarendon, 1985), p.364. See also *R. v Kennedy (Simon)* [2007] UKHL 38; [2008] 1 A.C. 269, per Lord Bingham of Cornhill at [14].

[66] *MacAngus (Kevin) v HM Advocate; Kane (Michael Alexander) v HM Advocate* [2009] HCJAC 8; 2009 S.L.T. 137, per the Lord Justice-General (Hamilton) at [48].

the causal inquiry to the question of whether B's conduct would have occurred but for A's actions.[67] The position as regards older children under s.31 is less clear, but the best view may be that B's status as a child[68] means that their participation in sexual activity cannot be regarded as wholly voluntary, and so the causal enquiry can again be limited in this way.

In limited circumstances, an omission to intervene to prevent non-consensual conduct might amount to causing it.[69] If a parent has a legal duty to intervene to prevent harm being inflicted on their child,[70] they must similarly have an obligation to intervene to prevent sexual abuse. It would, however, be necessary to prove that they intended their omission to result in B's participation in the activity: apathy or indifference, however shocking, would not suffice. In practical terms, therefore, a prosecution for sexual coercion, or causing a child to participate in a sexual activity, on the basis of an omission is a relatively unlikely prospect.[71]

COERCING PERSONS INTO BEING, AND CAUSING CHILDREN TO BE, PRESENT DURING SEXUAL ACTIVITY

2.19 In its report, the Scottish Law Commission raised the issue of people being caused to watch sexual activity without their consent, expressing the view that:

"… just as being forced to participate in sexual activity is an invasion of a person's sexual autonomy so is being forced to watch such activity".[72]

The Commission recommended the creation of an offence of causing persons without their consent to be present during sexual activity[73] and corresponding child offences.[74] The offence of coercing a person into being present during sexual activity is defined in the following terms by s.5 of the 2009 Act[75]:

"(1) If a person ('A')—
    (a)   without another person ('B') consenting, and
    (b)   without any reasonable belief that B consents,

---

[67] In *R. v Devonald (Stephen)* [2008] EWCA Crim 527 (concerning the analogous English offence under the Sexual Offences Act 2003 s.4) the defendant (a 37-year-old male) had purported, via the internet, to be a 20-year-old female in order to persuade a 16-year-old boy to masturbate in front of a webcam. It was accepted that he had caused the boy's behaviour and the appeal turned on the question of whether this behaviour was to be regarded as consensual: it was held that it was not. It is at least arguable that if his conduct was consensual it was not caused, but the point (which could not in any event have assisted his appeal) was not argued.

[68] cf. *Khaliq (Raja Abdul) v HM Advocate*, 1984 J.C. 23. Although the fact of the complainers in that case being children was not essential to the validity of the charge, it was nevertheless relevant to the question of causation: see *Khaliq*, per the Lord Justice-General (Emslie) at 35 and *Ulhaq (Anwar) v HM Advocate*, 1991 S.L.T. 614, per the Lord Justice-General (Hope) at 615.

[69] For a contrary view, see Card, Gillespie and Hirst, *Sexual Offences*, para.3.176, but the authority cited there (*Price v Cromack* [1975] 1 W.L.R. 988) seems of limited assistance in this context.

[70] Thus potentially rendering them liable for homicide if the injury is fatal: see *Bone (Andrea Lorraine) v HM Advocate*, 2006 S.L.T. 164. On the general issue of omissions as causal factors, see Gordon, *Criminal Law*, para.4.56.

[71] In the same way that it is unlikely that murder could be established following the death of a child caused by omission (but not impossible: see *R. v Gibbins (Walter)* (1919) 13 Cr. App. R. 134).

[72] *Report*, para.3.55.

[73] *Report*, paras 3.55–3.61. It was noted that the issue had not been raised in the *Discussion Paper* or by consultees. As to the pre-2009 Act position, there seems to be no clear authority, although see Gordon, *Criminal Law*, para.36.09.

[74] See *Report*, Ch.4.

[75] This is unchanged from s.4 of the Commission's draft Bill (see *Report*, pp.140, 141) save that the definition of "sexual" which was formerly included in s.4 itself is now found in s.60(2) of the 2009 Act.

either intentionally engages in a sexual activity and for a purpose mentioned in subsection (2) does so in the presence of B or intentionally and for a purpose mentioned in that subsection causes B to be present while a third person engages in such an activity, then A commits an offence, to be known as the offence of coercing a person into being present during a sexual activity.

(2) The purposes are—
    (a) obtaining sexual gratification,
    (b) humiliating, distressing or alarming B.

(3) Without prejudice to the generality of subsection (1), the reference in that subsection—
    (a) to A engaging in a sexual activity in the presence of B, includes a reference to A engaging in it in a place in which A can be observed by B other than by B looking at an image, and
    (b) to B being present while a third person engages in such an activity, includes a reference to B being in a place from which the third person can be so observed by B."

The offence carries a maximum penalty, on summary conviction, of 12 months' imprisonment and/or a fine not exceeding the statutory maximum and, on conviction on indictment, of imprisonment for a term not exceeding 10 years and/or a fine.[76] Six offences are specified as possible alternative verdicts.[77] The offence may be committed outwith the United Kingdom where A is a UK national or resident and B is under the age of 18.[78]

There are modified versions of this offence in respect of both older and young children (ss.32 and 22 respectively, which are discussed immediately below). Both of these offences, however, are based simply on causing the child to be present during sexual activity: there is no issue of consent on the child's part. In a similar manner to the offence of sexual coercion,[79] it follows that where it is alleged that an older child has been coerced into being present during sexual activity, s.5 is the appropriate charge, with s.32 available as an alternative verdict. By contrast, causing a younger child to be present during sexual activity should result in a charge under s.21 without any inquiry into any issue of "consent".

Modified offence in respect of older children

An offence of, "causing an older child to be present during a sexual activity" **2.20** is created by s.32 of the 2009 Act. The elements of this offence are identical to those for the s.5 offence, save that B must be an older child, A must have attained the age of 16 and there is no issue of consent (or reasonable belief therein). The proximity of age defence under s.39 (that is, that the difference between A's age and B's age did not exceed two years) is available,[80] and the general defence of reasonable mistake as to age applies.[81]

This offence carries a maximum penalty, on summary conviction, of 12

---

[76] 2009 Act Sch.2.

[77] 2009 Act Sch.3. These are: sexual coercion (s.4); coercing a person into looking at a sexual image (s.6); communicating indecently (s.7(1)); causing a person to see or hear an indecent communication (s.7(2)); causing an older child to participate in a sexual activity (s.31); sexual exposure (s.8); or assault at common law. It is perhaps surprising that the s.4 offence is an implied alternative verdict, given that it is a potentially more serious offence with a higher maximum penalty. Quaere whether it would be legitimate to impose a sentence of more than five years' imprisonment if A were charged under s.5 but convicted under s.4.

[78] 2009 Act s.55, Sch.4 Pt 2. On extraterritorial jurisdiction, see above, para.1.39.

[79] See above, para.2.15.

[80] 2009 Act s.39(3). See above, para.1.18.

[81] On this defence, see above, para.1.21.

months' imprisonment and/or a fine not exceeding the statutory maximum and, on conviction on indictment, of 10 years' imprisonment and/or a fine.[82] Four offences are specified as possible alternative verdicts.[83] The offence may be committed outwith the United Kingdom where A is a UK national or resident.[84]

Modified offence in respect of young children

2.21 An offence of, "causing a young child to be present during a sexual activity" is created by s.22 of the 2009 Act.[85] The elements of this offence are identical to those for the s.5 offence, save that B must be a young child and there is no issue of consent (or reasonable belief therein). It is no defence that A believed B had attained the age of 13 years.[86]

This offence carries a maximum penalty, on summary conviction, of 12 months' imprisonment and/or a fine not exceeding the statutory maximum and, on conviction on indictment, of imprisonment for a term not exceeding 10 years and/or a fine.[87] Eleven offences are specified as possible alternative verdicts.[88] The offence may be committed outwith the United Kingdom where A is a UK national or resident.[89]

The elements of the offences

2.22 The principal elements of these offences are mostly ones which are common to the scheme of the 2009 Act as a whole.[90] The issue of causation is discussed above in relation to the offences of sexual coercion and causing children to participate in sexual activity.[91] Two points about specific aspects of the offences should be noted. First, the required purpose (sexual gratification or humiliating, distressing or alarming B) must exist in relation to B's presence.[92] Where the charge is based on A's participation in a sexual act, it is not enough to show that A acted for sexual gratification in engaging in the sexual act itself.[93] Secondly, there is no requirement that B actually observe the act: it suffices that they were in a position to observe it.[94]

COERCING PERSONS INTO, AND CAUSING CHILDREN TO LOOK AT, SEXUAL IMAGES

2.23 The rationale for these offences is the same as those relating to coercing per-

---

[82] 2009 Act Sch.2.
[83] 2009 Act Sch.3. These are: causing an older child to participate in a sexual activity (s.31); causing an older child to look at a sexual image (s.33); communicating indecently with an older child (s.34(1)); causing an older child to see or hear an indecent communication (s.34(2)); and sexual exposure to an older child (s.35). As with the s.5 offence, this creates the oddity of an alternative verdict with a higher maximum sentence than the index offence: see above, fn.77.
[84] 2009 Act s.55, Sch.4 Pt 2. On extraterritorial jurisdiction, see above, para.1.39.
[85] See *Report*, paras 4.21–4.31.
[86] 2009 Act s.27. See above, para.1.20.
[87] 2009 Act Sch.2.
[88] 2009 Act Sch.3. These are: causing a young child to participate in a sexual activity (s.21); causing a young child to look at a sexual image (s.23); communicating indecently with a young child (s.24(1)); causing a young child to see or hear an indecent communication (s.24(2)); sexual exposure to a young child (s.25); causing an older child to participate in a sexual activity (s.31); causing an older child to be present during a sexual activity (s.32); causing an older child to look at a sexual image (s.33); communicating indecently with an older child (s.34(1)); causing an older child to see or hear an indecent communication (s.34(2)); and sexual exposure to an older child (s.35). As with the s.5 offence, this creates the oddity of an alternative verdict with a higher maximum sentence than the index offence: see above, fn.77.
[89] 2009 Act s.55, Sch.4 Pt 2. On extraterritorial jurisdiction, see above, para.1.39.
[90] See above, paras 1.01–1.14 and 1.22.
[91] See above, para.2.18.
[92] Seeking to humiliate, distress or alarm a third party, not present at the time of the act, would be insufficient for the offence.
[93] The point is discussed by Brown, *Sexual Offences (Scotland) Act 2009*, pp.27, 48 and 57.
[94] As the Scottish Law Commission specifically recommended: *Report*, para.3.60.

sons into being (or causing children to be) present during sexual activity, and the Scottish Law Commission accordingly grouped the relevant recommendations together in their report.[95] The offence of coercing a person into looking at a sexual image is defined in the following terms by s.6 of the 2009 Act[96]:

> "(1) If a person ('A') intentionally and for a purpose mentioned in subsection (2) causes another person ('B')—
>   (a) without B consenting, and
>   (b) without any reasonable belief that B consents,
> to look at a sexual image, then A commits an offence, to be known as the offence of coercing a person into looking at a sexual image.
>   (2) The purposes are—
>   (a) obtaining sexual gratification,
>   (b) humiliating, distressing or alarming B.
>   (3) For the purposes of subsection (1), a sexual image is an image (produced by whatever means and whether or not a moving image) of—
>   (a) A engaging in a sexual activity or of a third person or imaginary person so engaging,
>   (b) A's genitals or the genitals of a third person or imaginary person."

The offence carries a maximum penalty, on summary conviction, of 12 months' imprisonment and/or a fine not exceeding the statutory maximum and, on conviction on indictment, of imprisonment for a term not exceeding 10 years and/ or a fine.[97] Six offences are specified as possible alternative verdicts.[98] The offence may be committed outwith the United Kingdom where A is a UK national or resident and B is under the age of 18.[99]

There are modified versions of this offence in respect of both older and young children (ss.33 and 23 respectively, which are discussed immediately below). Both of these offences, however, are based simply on causing the child to look at a sexual image: there is no issue of consent on the child's part. It follows that where it is alleged that an older child has been coerced into looking at a sexual image, s.6 is the appropriate charge, with s.33 available as an alternative verdict.[100]

Modified offence in respect of older children

An offence of, "causing an older child to look at a sexual image" is created by **2.24** s.33 of the 2009 Act. The elements of this offence are identical to those for the s.6 offence, save that B must be an older child, A must have attained the age of 16 and there is no issue of consent (or reasonable belief therein). The proximity of age defence under s.39 (that is, that the difference between A's age and B's

---

[95] See *Report*, para.3.61.

[96] This is broadly similar to s.5 of the Commission's draft Bill (see *Report*, pp.140, 141), save that the definition of "sexual" which was formerly included in s.5 itself is now found in s.60(2) of the 2009 Act. More significantly, the Commission's definition of sexual image encompassed only images of individuals engaging in sexual activity: the relevant section of the Bill was amended on its progress through Parliament so as to bring images of genitalia within the scope of the offence.

[97] 2009 Act Sch.2.

[98] 2009 Act Sch.3. These are: sexual coercion (s.4); coercing a person into being present during a sexual activity (s.5); communicating indecently (s.7(1)); causing a person to see or hear an indecent communication (s.7(2)); causing an older child to participate in a sexual activity (s.31); sexual exposure (s.8); or assault at common law. The inclusion of the s.4 offence is somewhat surprising: see above, fn.77.

[99] 2009 Act s.55, Sch.4 Pt 2. On extraterritorial jurisdiction, see above, para.1.39.

[100] The relationship between the offences is similar to that discussed in respect of sexual coercion: see above, para.2.15.

age did not exceed two years) is available,[101] and the general defence of reasonable mistake as to age applies.[102]

This offence carries a maximum penalty, on summary conviction, of 12 months' imprisonment and/or a fine not exceeding the statutory maximum and, on conviction on indictment, of 10 years' imprisonment and/or a fine.[103] Four offences are specified as possible alternative verdicts.[104] The offence may be committed outwith the United Kingdom where A is a UK national or resident.[105]

Modified offence in respect of young children

2.25 An offence of, "causing a young child to look at a sexual image" is created by s.23 of the 2009 Act.[106] The elements of this offence are identical to those for the s.6 offence, save that B must be a young child and there is no issue of consent (or reasonable belief therein). It is no defence that A believed B had attained the age of 13 years.[107]

This offence carries a maximum penalty, on summary conviction, of 12 months' imprisonment and/or a fine not exceeding the statutory maximum and, on conviction on indictment, of imprisonment for a term not exceeding 10 years and/or a fine.[108] Eleven offences are specified as possible alternative verdicts.[109] The offence may be committed outwith the United Kingdom where A is a UK national or resident.[110]

The elements of the offences

2.26 The principal elements of these offences are mostly ones which are common to the scheme of the 2009 Act as a whole.[111] It should be noted that the *nomen juris* of the s.6 offence is misleading: there is no requirement that B actually be "coerced" into looking at the image. It would be sufficient, for example, for A to take B by surprise.[112]

INDECENT COMMUNICATIONS

2.27 The Scottish Law Commission recommended that offences of indecent communication be created, on the basis that making indecent communications with someone without their consent amounts to a violation of their sexual autonomy.[113] The 2009 Act includes offences which are defined in exactly the terms proposed by the Commission.

---

[101] 2009 Act s.39(3). See above, para.1.18.
[102] On this defence, see above, para.1.21.
[103] 2009 Act Sch.2.
[104] 2009 Act Sch.3. These are: causing an older child to participate in a sexual activity (s.31); causing an older child to be present during a sexual activity (s.33); communicating indecently with an older child (s.34(1)); causing an older child to see or hear an indecent communication (s.34(2)); and sexual exposure to an older child (s.35).
[105] 2009 Act s.55, Sch.4 Pt 2. On extraterritorial jurisdiction, see above, para.1.39.
[106] See *Report*, paras 4.21–4.31.
[107] 2009 Act s.27. See above, para.1.20.
[108] 2009 Act Sch.2.
[109] 2009 Act Sch.3. These are: causing a young child to participate in a sexual activity (s.21); causing a young child to be present during a sexual activity (s.22); communicating indecently with a young child (s.24(1)); sexual exposure to a young child (s.25); causing an older child to participate in a sexual activity (s.31); causing an older child to be present during a sexual activity (s.32); causing an older child to look at a sexual image (s.33); communicating indecently with an older child (s.34(1)); causing an older child to see or hear a sexual communication (s.34(2)); and sexual exposure to an older child (s.35).
[110] 2009 Act s.55, Sch.4 Pt 2. On extraterritorial jurisdiction, see above, para.1.39.
[111] See above, paras 1.01–1.14 and 1.22.
[112] See Brown, *Sexual Offences (Scotland) Act 2009*, pp.27, 28.
[113] *Report*, paras 3.62, 3.63.

Communicating indecently

The offence of communicating indecently under s.7(1) of the 2009 Act is com- **2.28**
mitted where the following elements are present:

 (1) A, "sends, by whatever means, a sexual written communication to or
 directs, by whatever means, a sexual verbal communication at" B;
 (2) The communication is intentional and for the purpose of either sexual
 gratification or humiliating, distressing or alarming B; and
 (3) The communication is sent, "without B consenting to its being so
 sent or directed" and A acts without any reasonable belief that B
 consents.

Five alternative verdicts are specified.[114]

Modifications in respect of children

Where B is an older child, the offence of communicating indecently with an **2.29**
older child under s.34(1) will be committed where items (1) and (2) alone are
present. This offence can only be committed where A has attained the age of
16 years, and it may be a defence that A reasonably believed B to have attained
that age.[115] The proximity of age defence under s.39 (that is, that the difference
between A's age and B's age did not exceed two years) is available.[116] Five
alternative verdicts are specified.[117]

 Where B is a young child, the offence of communicating indecently with
a young child under s.24(1) will be committed where items (1) and (2) are
present. Mistake as to B's age is not a defence.[118] Eleven alternative verdicts
are specified.[119]

Causing a person to see or hear an indecent communication

The offence of causing a person to see or hear an indecent communication **2.30**
under s.7(2) of the 2009 Act is committed where the following elements are
present:

 (1) A causes B, "to see or hear, by whatever means, a sexual written
 communication or sexual verbal communication";
 (2) The communication is intentional and for the purpose of either sexual
 gratification or humiliating, distressing or alarming B; and
 (3) B is caused to see or hear the communication without consenting to
 doing so, and A acts without any reasonable belief that B consents.

Five alternative verdicts are specified.[120]

---

[114] 2009 Act Sch.3. These are: sexual coercion (s.4); coercing a person into being present during
a sexual activity (s.5); coercing a person into looking at a sexual image (s.6); causing a person to
see or hear an indecent communication (s.7(2)); and sexual exposure (s.8).

[115] 2009 Act s.39. See above, para.1.21.

[116] 2009 Act s.39(3). See above, para.1.18.

[117] 2009 Act Sch.3. These are: causing an older child to participate in a sexual activity (s.31);
causing an older child to be present during a sexual activity (s.32); causing an older child to look
at a sexual image (s.33); causing an older child to see or hear an indecent communication (s.34(2));
and sexual exposure to an older child (s.35).

[118] 2009 Act s.27. See above, para.1.20.

[119] 2009 Act Sch.3. These are: causing a young child to participate in a sexual activity (s.21);
causing a young child to be present during a sexual activity (s.22); causing a young child to look
at a sexual image (s.23); causing a young child to see or hear an indecent communication (s.23);
sexual exposure to a young child (s.25); causing an older child to participate in a sexual activity
(s.31); causing an older child to be present during a sexual activity (s.32); causing an older child
to look at a sexual image (s.33); communicating indecently with an older child (s.34(1)); causing
an older child to see or hear an indecent communication (s.34(2)); and sexual exposure to an older
child (s.35).

[120] 2009 Act Sch.3. These are: sexual coercion (s.4); coercing a person into being present during
a sexual activity (s.5); coercing a person into looking at a sexual image (s.6); communicating
indecently (s.7); and sexual exposure (s.8).

Modifications in respect of children

2.31 Where B is an older child, the offence of causing an older child to see or hear an indecent communication under s.34(2) will be committed where items (1) and (2) alone are present. This offence can only be committed where A has attained the age of 16 years, and it may be a defence that A reasonably believed B to have attained that age.[121] The proximity of age defence under s.39 (that is, that the difference between A's age and B's age did not exceed two years) is available.[122] Five alternative verdicts are specified.[123]

Where B is a young child, the offence of causing a young child to see or hear an indecent communication under s.24(2) will be committed where items (1) and (2) are present. Mistake as to B's age is not a defence.[124] Eleven alternative verdicts are specified.[125]

Penalties, jurisdiction and alternative verdicts

2.32 The maximum penalty for all six offences of indecent communication is identical: on summary conviction, imprisonment for a term not exceeding 12 months and/or a fine not exceeding the statutory maximum, and on conviction on indictment, imprisonment for a term not exceeding 10 years and/or a fine.[126] All the offences may be committed outwith the United Kingdom where A is a UK national or resident and B is under the age of 18.[127]

One peculiar omission from the scheme of alternative verdicts (which are noted individually above in respect of each offence) is that the equivalent "older child" offences are not specified as alternative verdicts where one of the general offences under s.7 is charged. That is unfortunate. Where such conduct is alleged to have been committed in respect of an older child without the older child's consent, the appropriate course of action would seem to be to proceed under s.7 but charging the equivalent s.34 offence in the alternative.[128] Although all offences carry the same maximum penalty, the difference between the two offences is important in that a conviction under s.7 makes the absence of B's consent an element of the offence.[129] It would be improper to pass sentence under s.34 on the basis that B did not consent.[130]

---

[121] 2009 Act s.39. See above, para.1.21.

[122] 2009 Act s.39(3). See above, para.1.18.

[123] 2009 Act Sch.3. These are: causing an older child to participate in a sexual activity (s.31); causing an older child to be present during a sexual activity (s.32); causing an older child to look at a sexual image (s.33); communicating indecently with an older child (s.34); and sexual exposure to an older child (s.35).

[124] 2009 Act s.27. See above, para.1.20.

[125] 2009 Act Sch.3. These are: causing a young child to participate in a sexual activity (s.21); causing a young child to be present during a sexual activity (s.22); causing a young child to look at a sexual image (s.23); communicating indecently with a young child (s.24); sexual exposure to a young child (s.25); causing an older child to participate in a sexual activity (s.31); causing an older child to be present during a sexual activity (s.32); causing an older child to look at a sexual image (s.33); communicating indecently with an older child (s.34(1)); causing an older child to see or hear an indecent communication (s.34(2)); and sexual exposure to an older child (s.35).

[126] 2009 Act Sch.1.

[127] 2009 Act s.55, Sch.4 Pt 2. On extraterritorial jurisdiction, see above, para.1.39. B will of course always be under the age of 18 where the s.24 and s.34 offences are concerned.

[128] And as proximity of age is a complete defence to a charge under s.34, there will be no alternative open to the Crown other than to use s.7 where non-consensual indecent communication is alleged between two parties the difference between whose ages does not exceed two years (except where one party is a young child).

[129] This is presumably why a verdict under s.7 is not specified as an alternative verdict where an offence under s.34 is charged: the s.34 charge would not give fair notice that the accused was liable to be convicted of an offence implying non-consensual activity.

[130] cf. *McDade v HM Advocate*, 1998 S.L.T. 68.

Elements of the offences

The terminology "indecency" in the nomen juris for each offence is mislead- **2.33** ing, as indecency is not something which must be proven in respect of any of these offences. Instead, it must be proved that the communication is "sexual", a concept which runs throughout the Act.[131] The other elements of the offences are similarly common to the scheme of the 2009 Act as a whole, save for the references to communications. These are defined as follows[132]:

> "'written communication' means a communication in whatever written form, and without prejudice to that generality includes a communication which comprises writings of a person other than A (as for example a passage in a book or magazine), and
>
> 'verbal communication' means a communication in whatever verbal form, and without prejudice to that generality includes—
> (a) a communication which comprises sounds of sexual activity (whether actual or simulated), and
> (b) a communication by means of sign language."

There is no requirement that B actually appreciates the sexual nature of the communication, or indeed—where the s.7(1) offence is concerned—knows of the communication at all. If A sends B a sexual communication which is intercepted by a third party, the offence is still committed by virtue of the communication having been sent. The s.7(1) offence requires only that a communication (if written) be *sent* to or (if verbal) *directed at* B, not that there be actual communication.[133]

The issue of consent poses special difficulties in this context. Suppose that A and B are in a relationship, and A wishes to send B a sexual communication by means of a text message. Is this a criminal offence unless A first sends B a message saying, "can I send you a sexual text message?" To avoid absurdity, the relevant question must be whether A and B's relationship is of such a nature as to imply continuing consent to communication of this nature until one of the parties chooses to withdraw it, withdrawal itself being something which might be achieved by implication.[134]

SEXUAL EXPOSURE

The exposure of one's genitalia, as the Scottish Law Commission observed,[135] **2.34** can involve two very different types of wrong (although it should be noted that the same action of exposure could involve both wrongs simultaneously). It may be an offence against public order, in which case it falls within the ambit of the common law offence of public indecency,[136] or breach of the peace.[137] Alternatively, it may be an offence against a particular individual, but in the latter case it is not clear what crime (if any) was committed prior to the 2009 Act where the person to whom the exposure was made was an adult.[138]

---

[131] As such, it is discussed above, at para.1.01.

[132] 2009 Act s.7(4). The same definition is repeated in ss.24(4) and 34(4).

[133] cf. Brown, *Sexual Offences (Scotland) Act 2009*, p.31, who observes that B's sexual autonomy—which the offence is designed to protect—is not interfered with in such a case.

[134] See also Brown, *Sexual Offences (Scotland) Act 2009*, pp.29, 30.

[135] See *Report*, para.5.31.

[136] See *Webster v Dominick*, 2005 1 J.C. 65. It appears that this form of the offence of public indecency can be committed recklessly: see *Usai (Enrico) v Russell*, 2000 J.C. 144; James Chalmers and Christopher Gane, "The Aftermath of Shameless Indecency" (2003) 8 S.L.P.Q. 310.

[137] See Gordon, *Criminal Law*, para.36.14. See also the Civic Government (Scotland) Act 1982 s.47 (offence of urinating or defecating, "in such circumstances as to cause, or to be likely to cause, annoyance to any other person").

[138] See Gordon, *Criminal Law*, para.36.13.

The Commission recommended that such conduct be clearly designated as a sexual offence,[139] and the offence of sexual exposure is accordingly defined by s.8 of the 2009 Act in the following terms:

"(1) If a person ('A')—
    (a)   without another person ('B') consenting, and
    (b)   without any reasonable belief that B consents,

intentionally and for a purpose mentioned in subsection (2), exposes A's genitals in a sexual manner to B with the intention that B will see them, then A commits an offence, to be known as the offence of sexual exposure.

    (2) The purposes are—
    (a)   obtaining sexual gratification,
    (b)   humiliating, distressing or alarming B."

The offence carries a maximum penalty, on summary conviction, of 12 months' imprisonment and/or a fine not exceeding the statutory maximum and, on conviction on indictment, of imprisonment for a term not exceeding five years and/or a fine.[140] Two alternative verdicts are specified.[141] The offence may be committed outwith the United Kingdom where A is a UK national or resident and B is under the age of 18.[142]

Modified offence in respect of older children

2.35 Where B is an older child, the offence of sexual exposure to an older child under s.35 will be committed in the same circumstances at set out in s.8, save that the absence of consent (or reasonable belief therein) is irrelevant. This offence can only be committed where A has attained the age of 16 years, and it may be a defence that A reasonably believed B to have attained that age.[143] The proximity of age defence under s.39 (that is, that the difference between A's age and B's age did not exceed two years) is available.[144]

The offence carries a maximum penalty, on summary conviction, of 12 months' imprisonment and/or a fine not exceeding the statutory maximum and, on conviction on indictment, of imprisonment for a term not exceeding five years and/or a fine.[145] Two alternative verdicts are specified.[146] The offence may be committed outwith the United Kingdom where A is a UK national or resident.[147]

Modified offence in respect of young children

2.36 Where B is an young child, the offence of sexual exposure to a young child under s.25 will be committed in the same circumstances at set out in s.8, save that the absence of consent (or reasonable belief therein) is irrelevant. Mistake as to B's age is not a defence.[148]

The offence carries a maximum penalty, on summary conviction, of 12 months' imprisonment and/or a fine not exceeding the statutory maximum and, on conviction on indictment, of imprisonment for a term not exceeding 10

---

[139] *Report*, paras 5.15, 5.16.
[140] 2009 Act Sch.2.
[141] 2009 Act Sch.3. These are public indecency at common law and breach of the peace at common law.
[142] 2009 Act s.55, Sch.4 Pt 2. On extraterritorial jurisdiction, see above, para.1.39.
[143] 2009 Act s.39. See above, para.1.21.
[144] 2009 Act s.39(3). See above, para.1.18.
[145] 2009 Act Sch.2.
[146] 2009 Act Sch.3. These are public indecency at common law and breach of the peace at common law.
[147] 2009 Act s.55, Sch.4 Pt 2. On extraterritorial jurisdiction, see above, para.1.39.
[148] 2009 Act s.27. See above, para.1.20.

years and/or a fine.[149] Three alternative verdicts are specified.[150] The offence may be committed outwith the United Kingdom where A is a UK national or resident.[151]

Elements of the offences

The term "genitals" is not defined anywhere in the 2009 Act and must be re- **2.37**
garded as having its ordinary English language meaning. There is English authority to the effect that the genitals can be "exposed" even if no individual actually sees them,[152] but insofar as that authority suggests that exposure might be possible even if it was not possible for the genitalia to be seen it must surely be regarded as incorrect.[153] Even if actual sight by B is necessary for the crime to be committed (and the wording of the provision suggests that it is not), A would nonetheless be guilty of attempted sexual exposure if the other requirements of the offence were fulfilled.

One curious aspect of the offence is that the exposure must be, "in a sexual manner".[154] The ambiguity involved in the term "sexual" is discussed above,[155] where it was noted that one possible interpretation of the term is that it relates either to sexual gratification or to the sexual organs. But on that basis exposure of the genitalia would necessarily be "sexual" and this requirement meaningless. A narrower interpretation of "sexual" as restricted to sexual gratification would make no sense either as it would mean that the offence could not be committed where A's purpose fulfilled s.8(2)(b) but not s.8(2)(a).

The Commission did not explain what they intended the "in a sexual manner" requirement to mean beyond saying that it would be wrong for the offence to be restricted to cases where A acted for sexual gratification.[156] It seems to have favoured the requirement on the basis that it did not want the offence to cover conduct such as a man exposing his penis in a public place in order to urinate.[157] However, given that the offence is restricted to cases where A acted with the purpose of sexual gratification or humiliating, distressing or alarming B,[158] such cases are necessarily outwith the scope of the offence regardless of

---

[149] 2009 Act Sch.2.
[150] 2009 Act Sch.3. These are sexual exposure to an older child (s.35); public indecency at common law; and breach of the peace at common law.
[151] 2009 Act s.55, Sch.4 Pt 2. On extraterritorial jurisdiction, see above, para.1.39.
[152] *Hunt v DPP* [1990] Crim. L.R. 812, a prosecution under s.4 of the Vagrancy Act 1824 ("wilfully openly, lewdly, and obscenely exposing his person"). The relevant portions of s.4 of the 1824 Act were repealed by the Sexual Offences Act 2003 Sch.7 para.1.
[153] Rook and Ward, *Sexual Offences*, para.14.54. It is not clear that *Hunt* does in fact suggest this. Rook and Ward's criticism is based on J.C. Smith's commentary at [1990] Crim. L.R. 813, where it is noted that it is peculiar that the justices had been able to hold that Hunt's genitals were capable of being seen when a (short-sighted?) police officer had tried and failed to see them. Hunt's actions seemed to have been such as to make it clear to passers-by outside his window that he was masturbating (or at least seeking to give the impression of doing so), which might amount to public indecency or breach of the peace under Scots law; cf. *R. v Clark* [2005] 1 S.C.R. 6.
[154] cf. the equivalent English offence under s.66 of the Sexual Offences Act 2003, which has no such requirement.
[155] See above, para.1.01.
[156] *Report*, para.5.14.
[157] *Report*, para.5.15.
[158] This is different from the draft Bill in the Commission's report, s.7 of which provided that the offence could be committed where A was reckless as to whether B would be alarmed or distressed. However, it is not clear why the Commission made this recommendation or even whether this in fact represented its considered opinion. At para.5.14 of the *Report*, the Commission notes that consultees broadly agreed with its proposal (*Discussion Paper*, para.6.34) that, "it should be an offence for someone to expose his or her genitals with the purpose of causing alarm and distress" and then recommends (at para.5.16) that: "It should be an offence for a person to expose his or her genitals in a sexual manner with the intention of causing alarm or distress to someone else or being reckless as to causing these effects". The shift from "purpose" to "intention ... or being reckless" is neither acknowledged nor explained.

any "sexual manner" requirement. The consequence is that it is difficult to attribute any sensible meaning to this element of the offence.

Voyeurism

Background to the offence

2.38 The Scottish Law Commission did not consider the question of voyeurism in its review of sexual offences, and made no proposals in this regard. At common law, such behaviour could be dealt with as a breach of the peace,[159] although this approach suffers from three problems. First, it would be necessary to prove that A's behaviour as a voyeur was likely to be discovered at the time.[160] Secondly, a conviction for breach of the peace does not clearly identify A's conduct as a sexual offence.[161] Thirdly, although this was not an issue at the time the Commission conducted its review, the appeal court's recent decision that a "public element" is essential for a charge of breach of the peace to succeed would necessarily restrict the potential for this offence to be used in cases of voyeurism.[162]

In line with the Commission's report, the Sexual Offences (Scotland) Bill included no provisions on voyeurism when it was introduced into the Scottish Parliament. However, the Government amended the Bill at Stage 2 to include this offence, explaining that the provisions proposed were similar to those found in the Sexual Offences Act 2003.[163]

One difficulty with this sequence of events is that the rationale for having an offence of voyeurism has never been properly discussed or articulated. Is it designed to protect certain limited aspects of B's privacy from intentional intrusion (in which case A's motive may be irrelevant) or should it encompass only those persons who act with certain lewd motives (and may perhaps be liable to commit more serious sexual offences)?[164]

The English legislation derives from proposals in the earlier Home Office review of sex offences, which proposed a very broad offence of observing someone without their knowledge or consent in circumstances where they had a reasonable expectation of privacy.[165] Such an offence would not be a sexual one (although it would encompass sexual wrongdoing) and would have almost certainly been over-broad.[166] The subsequent English legislation was far narrower in its terms and is restricted to cases where A acts for sexual gratification, which has been trenchantly criticised (it hardly seems to make much difference if A instead acts to humiliate the victim).[167]

The Scottish legislation avoids that particular defect by providing that the offence can be committed either where A acts for sexual gratification or for

---

[159] See, e.g. *McDougall v Dochree (Peter John)*, 1992 J.C. 154.

[160] See *McDougall v Dochree*, 1992 J.C. 154; *Thompson v MacPhail*, 1989 S.L.T. 637. The point, however, appears to have been overlooked in *Bryce (Robert Kenneth) v Normand*, 1997 S.L.T. 1351.

[161] Although the sex offender notification procedure would have been available on the basis that there was, "a significant sexual aspect to the offender's behaviour in committing the offence": Sexual Offences Act 2003 Sch.3 para.60.

[162] *Harris (Mark) v HM Advocate* [2009] HCJAC 80; 2009 S.L.T. 1078.

[163] See Brown, *Sexual Offences (Scotland) Act 2009*, p.33. This is perhaps unfortunate, as the English provisions have been held up as a "prime example" of flawed drafting: J.R. Spencer, "The Drafting of Criminal Legislation: Need it be so Impenetrable?" [2008] C.L.J. 585, 590.

[164] James Chalmers, "Two Problems in the Sexual Offences (Scotland) Bill", 2009 S.C.L. 553, 555.

[165] Home Office, *Setting the Boundaries*, 2000, para.8.3.10.

[166] The review acknowledged that it might inappropriately restrict the freedom of the press: see Home Office, *Setting the Boundaries*, 2000, para.8.3.10.

[167] Spencer, "The Drafting of Criminal Legislation" [2008] C.L.J. 585, 591.

the purpose of humiliating, distressing or alarming B.[168] It replicates another defect, which is that because it is limited to cases where B is observed "doing a private act", neither the English nor the Scottish legislation addresses the practice referred to as "upskirting" where A surreptitiously aims a camera up B's skirt to film her underclothes.[169] The English courts have been constrained to deal with such cases by way of the offence of outraging public decency.[170] In Scotland, the Government has proposed amendments to the 2009 Act which would expand the scope of s.9 (and the associated child offences) to encompass such conduct: at the time of writing, these were under consideration by the Parliament as part of the Criminal Justice and Licensing (Scotland) Bill.[171] As it could not be assumed that these amendments would pass into legislation in their original form, they are not considered further here.

Voyeurism as defined under the 2009 Act

Section 9 of the 2009 Act defines the offence of voyeurism in the following terms: **2.39**

"(1) A person ('A') commits an offence, to be known as the offence of voyeurism, if A does any of the things mentioned in subsections (2) to (5).
(2) The first thing is that A—
(a)   without another person ('B') consenting, and
(b)   without any reasonable belief that B consents,
for a purpose mentioned in subsection (6) observes B doing a private act.
(3) The second thing is that A—
(a)   without another person ('B') consenting, and
(b)   without any reasonable belief that B consents,
operates equipment with the intention of enabling A or another person ('C'), for a purpose mentioned in subsection (7), to observe B doing a private act.
(4) The third thing is that A—
(a)   without another person ('B') consenting, and
(b)   without any reasonable belief that B consents,
records B doing a private act with the intention that A or another person ('C'), for a purpose mentioned in subsection (7), will look at an image of B doing the act.
(5) The fourth thing is that A—
(a)   installs equipment, or
(b)   constructs or adapts a structure or part of a structure with the intention of enabling A or another person to do an act referred to in subsection (2), (3) or (4).
(6) The purposes referred to in subsection (2) are—
(a)   obtaining sexual gratification,
(b)   humiliating, distressing or alarming B.

---

[168] This is still not entirely satisfactory: what if B is a child and A acts to humiliate, distress or alarm B's parent? It may be that such behaviour is too far removed from the purpose for which the offence has been created to fall within its scope, but this is precisely why the absence of any articulated purpose is so problematic.

[169] See Alisdair A. Gillespie, "'Up-skirts' and 'Down Blouses': Voyeurism and the Law" [2008] Crim. L.R. 370.

[170] See *R. v Hamilton (Simon Austin)* [2007] EWCA Crim 2062; [2008] Q.B. 224. In Scotland, breach of the peace might be applicable in some cases, but that would require proof that A's act was likely to be seen. Where this is not the case, and A's activity comes to light only because his recordings of photographs are later discovered, a breach of the peace charge would be difficult to sustain: see Chalmers, "Two Problems in the Sexual Offences (Scotland) Bill", 2009 S.C.L. 553, 554, 555.

[171] They were included in the first grouping of amendments for Stage 2, available at *http://www.scottish.parliament.uk/s3/bills/24-CrimJustLc/index.htm* [Accessed May 23, 2010].

(7) The purposes referred to in subsections (3) and (4) are—
(a)   obtaining sexual gratification (whether for A or C),
(b)   humiliating, distressing or alarming B."

The offence carries a maximum penalty, on summary conviction, of 12 months' imprisonment and/or a fine not exceeding the statutory maximum and, on conviction on indictment, of imprisonment for a term not exceeding five years and/or a fine.[172] The sole available alternative verdict is breach of the peace at common law.[173] The offence may be committed outwith the United Kingdom where A is a UK national or resident and B is under the age of 18.[174]

Modified offence in respect of older children

2.40   Where B is an older child, the offence of voyeurism towards an older child under s.36 will be committed in the same circumstances at set out in s.9, save that the absence of consent (or reasonable belief therein) is irrelevant. This offence can only be committed where A has attained the age of 16 years, and it may be a defence that A reasonably believed B to have attained that age.[175] The proximity of age defence under s.39 (that is, that the difference between A's age and B's age did not exceed two years) is available.[176]

The offence carries a maximum penalty, on summary conviction, of 12 months' imprisonment and/or a fine not exceeding the statutory maximum and, on conviction on indictment, of imprisonment for a term not exceeding five years and/or a fine.[177] The sole available alternative verdict is breach of the peace at common law.[178] The offence may be committed outwith the United Kingdom where A is a UK national or resident.[179]

Modified offence in respect of young children

2.41   Where B is a young child, the offence of voyeurism towards to a young child under s.26 will be committed in the same circumstances as set out in s.9, save that the absence of consent (or reasonable belief therein) is irrelevant. Mistake as to B's age is not a defence.[180]

The offence carries a maximum penalty, on summary conviction, of 12 months' imprisonment and/or a fine not exceeding the statutory maximum and, on conviction on indictment, of imprisonment for a term not exceeding 10 years and/or a fine.[181] Two alternative verdicts are specified.[182] The offence may be committed outwith the United Kingdom where A is a UK national or resident.[183]

Elements of the offence

2.42   Voyeurism is what may be described as a "differentiated offence"[184]: that is, it

---

[172]   2009 Act Sch.2.
[173]   2009 Act Sch.3.
[174]   2009 Act s.55, Sch.4 Pt 2. On extraterritorial jurisdiction, see above, para.1.39.
[175]   2009 Act s.39. See above, para.1.21.
[176]   2009 Act s.39(3). See above, para.1.18.
[177]   2009 Act Sch.2.
[178]   2009 Act Sch.3.
[179]   2009 Act s.55, Sch.4 Pt 2. On extraterritorial jurisdiction, see above, para.1.39.
[180]   2009 Act s.27. See above, para.1.20.
[181]   2009 Act Sch.2.
[182]   2009 Act Sch.3. These are voyeurism towards an older child (s.36) and breach of the peace at common law.
[183]   2009 Act s.55, Sch.4 Pt 2. On extraterritorial jurisdiction, see above, para.1.39.
[184]   Victor Tadros, "Rape Without Consent" (2006) 26 O.J.L.S. 515, 517, 518.

is a single crime which can be committed in a number of different ways,[185] as set out in subss.(2)–(5) of the offence definition. Those elements of the offence which are not common to the scheme of the Act as a whole are defined in s.10, which provides as follows[186]:

"(1) For the purposes of section 9, a person is doing a private act if the person is in a place which in the circumstances would reasonably be expected to provide privacy, and—

(a)   the person's genitals, buttocks or breasts are exposed or covered only with underwear,

(b)   the person is using a lavatory, or

(c)   the person is doing a sexual act that is not of a kind ordinarily done in public.

(2) For the purposes of section 9(3), operating equipment includes enabling or securing its activation by another person without that person's knowledge.

(3) In section 9(5), 'structure' includes a tent, vehicle or vessel or other temporary or movable structure."

Section 10(1) is identical in its terms to an English provision[187] which was considered in *R. v Bassett*.[188] There, the Court of Appeal observed that a reasonable expectation of privacy did not require that a person was, "wholly enclosed or wholly sheltered from the possibility of being seen".[189] If someone were using changing rooms in a sporting facility, they might have, "no reasonable expectation of privacy from casual observation by other changing room users",[190] even if the observer derived sexual gratification from what they saw. But by contrast, the fact that individuals using the showers in these changing rooms would have no expectation of privacy from those passing by does not mean that they have no reasonable expectation of privacy from, "being spied upon by someone outside who has drilled a hole in the wall for the purpose".[191] The question, therefore, seems to be whether B has a reasonable expectation of privacy from observation of the mode engaged in by A. *Bassett* also holds that the word "breasts" in the statutory definition refers only to female breasts and not the exposed male chest.[192]

ADMINISTERING A SUBSTANCE FOR SEXUAL PURPOSES

It its report, the Scottish Law Commission noted that, "[o]ne way in which **2.43** someone may find herself having sex without her consent is where she had previously been given a stupefying substance",[193] and recommended that a specific offence should be created of administering a substance for sexual purposes, both to mark out the conduct concerned as intrinsically wrong and to ensure that criminal liability would be imposed even where there was no resulting sexual contact. Such an offence is created by s.11 of the 2009 Act.

At common law, drugging a person might (and still could be) charged as

---

[185] Some factual examples are set out in Rook and Ward, *Sexual Offences*, para.14.59.

[186] This section is applied to the child variants of the offence by the 2009 Act ss.26(8), 36(8).

[187] Sexual Offences Act 2003 s.68(1).

[188] *R. v Bassett (Kevin)* [2008] EWCA Crim 1174; [2009] 1 W.L.R. 1032.

[189] *R. v Bassett* [2009] 1 W.L.R. 1032, per Hughes L.J. at [7], referring to *R. v Swyer* [2007] EWCA Crim 204, where "marathon runners ... who had gone behind a hedge or into a shrubbery to urinate, had an expectation of privacy from being pursued and watched".

[190] *R. v Bassett* [2009] 1 W.L.R. 1032, per Hughes L.J. at [10].

[191] *R. v Bassett* [2009] 1 W.L.R. 1032, per Hughes L.J. at [10].

[192] *R. v Bassett* [2009] 1 W.L.R. 1032, per Hughes L.J. at [13]–[15].

[193] *Report*, para.3.64.

a form of causing real injury,[194] while there was a specific statutory offence under s.7(2)(c) of the Criminal Law (Consolidation) (Scotland) Act 1995 of applying, administering, or causing to be taken a substance by a woman or girl with the intent to stupefy or overpower her so as to enable any person to have unlawful sexual intercourse with her.[195]

Despite the potential existence of common law liability for drugging, the new statutory offence has the advantage of properly identifying A's conduct as a sexual offence. Section 11 is in the following terms[196]:

"(1) If a person ('A') intentionally administers a substance to, or causes a substance to be taken by, another person ('B')—
   (a)   without B knowing, and
   (b)   without any reasonable belief that B knows,
and does so for the purpose of stupefying or overpowering B, so as to enable any person to engage in a sexual activity which involves B, then A commits an offence, to be known as the offence of administering a substance for sexual purposes.

   (2) For the purposes of subsection (1), if A, whether by act or omission, induces in B a reasonable belief that the substance administered or taken is (either or both)—
   (a)   of a substantially lesser strength, or
   (b)   in a substantially lesser quantity,
than it is, any knowledge which B has (or belief as to knowledge which B has) that it is being administered or taken is to be disregarded."

The offence carries a maximum penalty, on summary conviction, of 12 months' imprisonment and/or a fine not exceeding the statutory maximum and, on conviction on indictment, of imprisonment for a term not exceeding five years and/or a fine.[197] No alternative verdicts are specified.[198] The offence may be committed outwith the United Kingdom where A is a UK national or resident and B is under the age of 18.[199]

Administration need not involve the application of direct physical force to B: for example, spraying CS gas in a person's face could amount to "administration".[200] However, the requirement that B must not know of the substance's administration means that the offence is in practice likely to be restricted to surreptitious administration, most obviously by placing the substance in a drink without B's knowledge. Because the offence is based on B's lack of knowledge and not the absence of B's consent,[201] forcing B to take a stupefying substance—although clearly criminal—does not constitute an offence under s.11.

The threshold of "stupefying or overpowering" is a strong one, and would not seem to encompass conduct which is aimed simply at lowering—rather than effectively removing—B's inhibitions. So, for example, if A buys B mixed drinks of double strength when B has requested single measures, al-

---

[194] Gordon, *Criminal Law*, para.29.48, where it is noted that fraud might also be a relevant charge.
[195] This offence is repealed by the 2009 Act Sch.6.
[196] This is unchanged from s.8 of the Commission's draft Bill (see *Report*, p.144) save that the definition of "sexual" which was formerly included in s.8 itself is now found in s.60(2) of the 2009 Act.
[197] 2009 Act Sch.2.
[198] 2009 Act Sch.3.
[199] 2009 Act s.55, Sch.4 Pt 2. On extraterritorial jurisdiction, see above, para.1.39.
[200] *R. v Gillard (Simon Paul)* (1988) 87 Cr. App. R. 189 (concerning the offence under s.24 of the Offences Against the Person Act 1861 of administering a noxious thing). See also *R. v Kennedy* [2008] 1 A.C. 269, per Lord Bingham of Cornhill at [10].
[201] In contrast to the equivalent English legislation: Sexual Offences Act 2003 s.61.

though s.11(2) would then be applicable, it would be difficult (perhaps depending on the overall quantity of alcohol involved) to show that A's intentions went so far as stupefying or overpowering B.

It is entirely irrelevant to this offence whether or not sexual activity follows on from A's conduct: the offence is complete at the point the substance is administered or taken.[202] It is equally irrelevant whether the substance was in fact capable of stupefying B: all that matters is B's intention in administering it. This is particularly important given that the effects of what are referred to as "date-rape drugs" can be overstated[203]: if A has acted on a false belief as to the potency of the substance he has utilised, this is no defence.

SEXUAL ACTIVITY WITH OLDER CHILDREN

Sections 28–30 of the Act create a series of offences concerning sexual activity **2.44** with older children. In their definitions, these provisions parallel the offences of rape (s.1),[204] sexual assault by penetration (s.2)[205] and sexual assault (s.3),[206] save that A must have attained the age of 16 years[207] and neither consent on B's part nor the absence of a reasonable belief in consent on the part of A is an element of the offence. They could therefore be regarded as modified versions of the ss.1–3 offences, but in practice the offences of, e.g. rape and consensual sexual intercourse with an older child are so distinct in their nature that they would normally be regarded as distinct offences denoting a very different type of wrongdoing.

These offences rationalise the earlier patchwork of common law and statutory rules in this area, with one significant change: prior to the 2009 Act, heterosexual activity with a boy who had attained the age of 14 but was not yet 16 was not in itself a criminal offence. This was because the common law offence of lewd, indecent and libidinous conduct applied only to boys under the age of 14.[208] The Scottish Law Commission considered this to be unsatisfactory, on the basis that the law should operate in a gender neutral fashion and that there should be, "no difference given to the protection of children because of their gender".[209]

The offences are as follows:

Having intercourse with an older child

Under s.28, this is committed where A, "with A's penis, penetrates to any ex- **2.45** tent, either intending to do so or reckless as to whether there is penetration, the vagina, anus or mouth" of B.[210] Three alternative verdicts are specified.[211] It

---

[202] Conversely, even if multiple sexual acts take place thereafter, only one crime has been committed in respect of the substance's administration, although the subsequent acts themselves may amount to separate offences. See *R. v Shillingford (Holly)* [1968] 1 W.L.R. 566.

[203] Emily Finch and Vanessa E. Munro, "Intoxicated Consent and the Boundaries of Drug Assisted Rape" [2003] Crim. L.R. 773, 775, 776.

[204] See above, para.2.02.

[205] See above, para.2.06.

[206] See above, para.2.10.

[207] Where A has not attained the age of 16 years, an offence may have been committed under s.37 of the 2009 Act (older children engaging in sexual conduct with each other). See below, para.2.49.

[208] That being in law the age of puberty. See Gordon, *Criminal Law*, para.36.09; *Report*, para.4.13. Homosexual activity with a boy under that age was an offence under s.13 of the Criminal Law (Consolidation) (Scotland) Act 1995. While the common law offence of lewd, indecent and libidinous conduct similarly applied only to girls under the age of puberty (12), s.6 of the 1995 Act created a statutory variant applicable to girls over 12 but under 16.

[209] *Report*, para.4.17; cf. Brown, *Sexual Offences (Scotland) Act 2009*, pp.63, 64.

[210] 2009 Act s.28.

[211] 2009 Act Sch.3. These are: engaging in penetrative sexual activity with or towards an older child (s.29); engaging in sexual activity with or towards an older child (s.30); and engaging while an older child in sexual conduct with or towards another older child (s.37).

may be a defence that A reasonably believed B to have attained the age of 16 years,[212] but the proximity of age defence is not available.[213]

Engaging in penetrative sexual activity with or towards an older child

2.46 Under s.29, this is committed where A, "with any part of A's body or anything else penetrates sexually to any extent, either intending to do so or reckless as to whether there is penetration, the vagina or anus" of B.[214] Two alternative verdicts are specified.[215] It may be a defence that A reasonably believed B to have attained the age of 16 years,[216] but the proximity of age defence is not available.[217]

Engaging in sexual activity with or towards an older child

2.47 Under s.30, this is committed where A does any of the following things[218]:

> "(a)   penetrates sexually, by any means and to any extent, either intending to do so or reckless as to whether there is penetration, the vagina, anus or mouth of B,
>
> (b)   intentionally or recklessly touches B sexually,
>
> (c)   engages in any other form of sexual activity in which A, intentionally or recklessly, has physical contact (whether bodily contact or contact by means of an implement and whether or not through clothing) with B,
>
> (d)   intentionally or recklessly ejaculates semen onto B,
>
> (e)   intentionally or recklessly emits urine or saliva onto B sexually."

One alternative verdict is specified.[219] It may be a defence that A reasonably believed B to have attained the age of 16 years.[220] The proximity of age defence under s.39 (that is, that the difference between A's age and B's age did not exceed two years) is available to a limited extent depending on the nature of the charge. As regards item (a), it is not available insofar as the charge is founded on, "penetration of B's vagina, anus or mouth with A's penis" or, "penetration of B's vagina or anus with A's mouth, tongue or teeth".[221]

As regards items (b) and (c), the proximity of age defence is not available insofar as the charge is founded on:

> "... sexual touching or other physical activity involving ... B's vagina, anus or penis being touched sexually by A's mouth ... A's vagina, anus or mouth being penetrated by B's penis [or] A's vagina, anus or penis being touched sexually by B's mouth".[222]

The proximity of age defence is available without restriction where the charge is founded on item (d) but is not available at all where it is founded on (e).[223]

---

[212]   2009 Act s.39. See above, para.1.21.

[213]   2009 Act s.39(3). See above, para.1.18.

[214]   2009 Act s.29(1). The reference to "penetration" includes penetration with A's penis: s.29(2). This means that where penetration is proved but there is doubt as to whether it was penile, A can be convicted of the s.29 offence rather than being acquitted on the basis that neither the s.28 nor the s.29 offence has been proven.

[215]   2009 Act Sch.3. These are: engaging in sexual activity with or towards an older child (s.30) and engaging while an older child in sexual conduct with or towards another older child (s.37).

[216]   2009 Act s.39. See above, para.1.21.

[217]   2009 Act s.39(3). See above, para.1.18.

[218]   2009 Act s.30(2).

[219]   2009 Act Sch.3. This is engaging while an older child in sexual conduct with or towards another older child (s.37).

[220]   2009 Act s.39. See above, para.1.21.

[221]   2009 Act s.39(4)(a).

[222]   2009 Act s.39(4)(b).

[223]   2009 Act s.39(4)(c).

(Why it should be available with regard to the ejaculation of semen but not the "sexual emission" of saliva on to B is unclear.)

Elements of the offences, penalties and jurisdiction

The elements of the offences are ones which are common to the scheme of the **2.48** 2009 Act as a whole.[224] The maximum penalty for all three of these offences is identical: on summary conviction, 12 months' imprisonment and/or a fine not exceeding the statutory maximum and, on conviction on indictment, of imprisonment for a term not exceeding 10 years and/or a fine.[225] All three offences may be committed outwith the United Kingdom where A is a UK national or resident.[226]

OLDER CHILDREN ENGAGING IN SEXUAL CONDUCT WITH EACH OTHER

Where both A and B are older children, A will be guilty under s.37(1) of the **2.49** offence of engaging while an older child in sexual conduct with or towards an older child if A does either of the following[227]:

> "(a) penetrates sexually, with A's penis and to any extent, either intending to do so or reckless as to whether there is penetration, the vagina, anus or mouth of B,
> (b) intentionally or recklessly touches the vagina, anus or penis of B sexually with A's mouth."

If B engages by consent in the conduct in question, then B is guilty under s.37(4) of the offence of engaging while an older child in consensual sexual conduct with another older child.[228]

The offence carries a maximum penalty, on summary conviction, of 12 months' imprisonment and/or a fine not exceeding the statutory maximum and, on conviction on indictment, of imprisonment for a term not exceeding 10 years and/or a fine.[229] No alternative verdicts are specified.[230] The offence may be committed outwith the United Kingdom where A is a UK national or resident.[231]

The elements of the offence are ones which are common to the scheme of the 2009 Act as a whole.[232] One curious aspect, which may be an accident of drafting, is that it must be proved that penile penetration of the vagina, anus or mouth is "sexual". This is not necessary in respect of other offences which are defined by reference to this conduct. The requirement seems redundant: such conduct is inherently sexual.[233]

ABUSE OF TRUST OFFENCES

The offence of sexual abuse of trust under the 2009 Act has its origins in the **2.50** Sexual Offences (Amendment) Act 2000, which lowered the age of consent for male homosexual acts from 18 to 16 under Scots law. This legislation was passed for the UK as a whole after it became clear that the former distinction between the two types of activity was in breach of the European Convention

---

[224] Some of them are specifically defined under s.38, but not in a manner which differs from the rest of the Act.
[225] 2009 Act Sch.2.
[226] 2009 Act s.55, Sch.4 Pt 2. On extraterritorial jurisdiction, see above, para.1.39.
[227] 2009 Act s.37(3).
[228] 2009 Act s.37(4).
[229] 2009 Act Sch.2.
[230] 2009 Act Sch.3.
[231] 2009 Act s.55, Sch.4 Pt 2. On extraterritorial jurisdiction, see above, para.1.39.
[232] Some of them are specifically defined under s.38, but not in a manner which differs from the rest of the Act.
[233] For discussion of the term "sexual", see above, para.1.01.

on Human Rights.[234] That Act created an offence of abuse of a position of trust, committed where A was in a (statutorily defined) position of trust in relation to B, A was over the age of 18 and B under that age, and A engaged in sexual activity with or towards B. The offence was created on a UK-wide basis but was subsequently replaced in English law by new provisions in the Sexual Offences Act 2003.

The 2009 Act retains this offence—now termed "sexual abuse of trust"— but with various modifications following on from the Scottish Law Commission's recommendations.[235] The Act also applies the same model to mentally disordered persons, creating an offence of, "sexual abuse of trust of a mentally disordered person".[236] These offences are considered separately below.

Sexual abuse of trust

2.51 Under s.42 of the 2009 Act, the offence of sexual abuse of trust is committed where A has attained the age of 18 years, B is under 18, A is in a position of trust in relation to B, and A, "intentionally engages in a sexual activity with or directed towards" B.

The offence carries a maximum penalty, on summary conviction, of 12 months' imprisonment and/or a fine not exceeding the statutory maximum and, on conviction on indictment, of imprisonment for a term not exceeding five years and/or a fine.[237] There are no offences specified as possible alternative verdicts.[238] The offence may be committed outwith the United Kingdom where A is a UK national or resident.[239]

Elements of the offence

2.52 The offence is one of strict liability as regards B's age and the existence of the position of trust.[240] The question of what is meant by a "sexual" activity is discussed above.[241] Beyond that, the only element of the offence which requires explanation is that of the position of trust itself. This exists when any one of five conditions set out in s.43 are satisfied. Subsections (2)–(6) are in the following terms:

> "(2) The first condition is that B is detained by virtue of an order of court or under an enactment in an institution and A looks after persons under 18 in that institution.
>
>   (3) The second condition is that B is resident in a home or other place in which accommodation is provided by a local authority under section 26(1) of the Children (Scotland) Act 1995 (c. 36) and A looks after persons under 18 in that place.

---

[234] *Sutherland v United Kingdom* (1997) 24 E.H.R.R. CD22. On the Act, see J.P. Burnside, "The Sexual Offences (Amendment) Act 2000: The Head of a 'Kiddy-Libber' and the Torso of a 'Child-Saver'?" [2001] Crim. L.R. 425. In fact, the Act did not quite achieve equalisation, because it remained the case in Scots law that no offence was committed by an adult woman engaging in sexual activity with a boy who had attained the age of 14, but the 2009 Act achieves full equalisation. See above, para.1.15.

[235] See *Report*, paras 4.126–4.134.

[236] 2009 Act s.46. See below, para.2.55.

[237] 2009 Act Sch.2.

[238] 2009 Act Sch.3. These are: coercing a person into being present during a sexual activity (s.5); coercing a person into looking at a sexual image (s.6); communicating indecently (s.7(1)); causing a person to see or hear an indecent communication (s.7(2)); causing an older child to participate in a sexual activity (s.31); or assault at common law.

[239] 2009 Act s.55, Sch.4 Pt 2. On extraterritorial jurisdiction, see above, para.1.39.

[240] cf. Brown, *Sexual Offences (Scotland) Act 2009*, p.72, who argues that this point is in doubt. However, the fact that a defence of reasonable belief that no position of trust existed is created by s.45(1)(b) of the 2009 Act must be a clear exclusion of mens rea by implication (on which see Gordon, *Criminal Law*, para.8.08).

[241] See above, para.1.01.

(4) The third condition is that B is accommodated and cared for in—
- (a)   a hospital,
- (b)   accommodation provided by an independent health care service,
- (c)   accommodation provided by a care home service,
- (d)   a residential establishment, or
- (e)   accommodation provided by a school care accommodation service or a secure accommodation service,

and A looks after persons under 18 in that place.

(5) The fourth condition is that B is receiving education at—
- (a)   a school and A looks after persons under 18 in that school, or
- (b)   a further or higher education institution and A looks after B in that institution.

(6) The fifth condition is that A—
- (a)   has any parental responsibilities or parental rights in respect of B,
- (b)   fulfils any such responsibilities or exercises any such rights under arrangement with a person who has such responsibilities or rights,
- (c)   had any such responsibilities or rights but no longer has such responsibilities or rights, or
- (d)   treats B as a child of A's family,

and B is a member of the same household as A."

"Looks after" means that A, "regularly cares for, teaches, trains, supervises or is in sole charge of" B.[242]

Defences

Four defences to the offence are established by s.45. These are as follows: A **2.53** reasonably believed that B had attained the age of 18; A reasonably believed that B was not a person in relation to whom A was in a position of trust; B was A's spouse or civil partner; or immediately before the position of trust came into being, a sexual relationship existed between A and B.

Some guidance on what is meant by reasonable belief as to B's age may be found by way of parallel with the provisions on reasonable mistake as to B's age in respect of offences against older children, which are discussed above.[243] The defence of reasonable belief in the absence of a relationship of trust is an odd one, because while A might have considered whether a relationship of trust existed and concluded that it did not, the far more likely scenario is that A simply does not know of the relationship's existence. Under the 2000 Act, the equivalent defence was that A:

> "… did not know, and could not reasonably have been expected to know, that B was a person in relation to whom he was in a position of trust".[244]

The Scottish Law Commission considered that this defence should continue to exist but—in what appears to have been an inadvertent decision rather than a deliberate change—formulated the relevant recommendation so as to lead to this change in wording.[245] If A was unaware of the relationship at the relevant time, then he should have in principle a defence if his *ignorance*—rather than belief—was reasonable, but this does depart from the literal wording of the statute.

---

[242] 2009 Act s.43(7). See s.44 for other definitions of the terms used in s.33.
[243] See above, para.1.21.
[244] Sexual Offences (Amendment) Act 2000 s.3(2)(b).
[245] See *Report*, paras 4.133, 4.134.

Abuse of trust under the Sexual Offences Act 2003: English jurisdiction over Scotland

2.54 In English law, the Sexual Offences Act 2003 creates a number of abuse of trust offences. Although these provisions have their roots in the same legislation as the Scottish ones, they are differently structured to the Scottish legislation, and the list of positions of trust differs from that in Scotland. Those differences are for the most part relatively technical, reflecting different drafting techniques and certain relationships which arise as a result of English legislation. The differences, however, potentially matter in Scotland because of a very unusual provision in the 2003 Act. Under s.20 of that Act, anything which would amount to an abuse of trust offence under the 2003 Act if done in England and Wales, "also constitutes that offence if done in Scotland". This seems to have been because of a concern that when the 2003 Act was passed, broadening the existing definition of "position of trust" for English law, the English provisions could be evaded by travel to Scotland.[246]

The jurisdictional provision is open to obvious criticisms as an usurpation of Scottish legislative authority, but it has some merits. First, these are offences over which there is a general extraterritorial jurisdiction where A is British,[247] and there is something rather unsatisfactory about jurisdictional rules which say—as the rules on extraterritorial jurisdiction generally do—that the English (or Scottish) courts have jurisdiction over an act which takes place anywhere in the world except Scotland (or England).[248] Secondly, some of the English positions of trust refer to positions to which A might be appointed under English legislation—some of which are appointments made by a court order—and while it is unsurprising that the Scottish legislation does not refer to those, that does not reflect a decision that sexual activity between persons within the relevant relationship should be lawful if the parties travel to Scotland.[249] However, neither point is a wholly satisfactory defence of the English rule.

There is probably only one real difference in principle between the definition of "position of trust" in the two jurisdictions, and it is narrow in scope. The 2003 Act creates a position of trust where:

> "A looks after persons under 18 who are receiving education at an educational institution and B is receiving, and A is not receiving, education at that institution".[250]

The Scottish Law Commission thought that a definition along these lines—as was previously found in Scots law[251]—was too broad in its scope, and the 2009 Act accordingly provides that insofar as further and higher education institutions are concerned, there will only be a relationship of trust where B is a stu-

---

[246] See Card, Gillespie and Hirst, *Sexual Offences*, para.2.104.

[247] Sexual Offences Act 2003 s.72. For the equivalent Scottish provisions, see above, para.1.39.

[248] Such rules are potentially rather problematic if there is any doubt as to whether the act took place in England or Scotland. For a discussion of the problem in relation to murder, where similar rules apply, see Michael Hirst, "Murder in England or Murder in Scotland?" (1995) 54 C.L.J. 488.

[249] See Sexual Offences Act 2003 s.21.

[250] Sexual Offences Act 2003 s.21(5). For the Scottish rule immediately prior to the 2009 Act, see s.4(5) of the Sexual Offences (Amendment) Act 2000: "A looks after persons under 18 who are receiving full-time education at an educational institution, and B is receiving such education at that institution." This is identical apart from the element of A not receiving education at the institution (which means that, for example, a postgraduate tutor is not in a position of trust in relation to an undergraduate) which appears in the 2003 Act. The 2000 Act's definition also applied in English law until it was replaced by the 2003 Act.

[251] Sexual Offences (Amendment) Act 2000 s.4.

dent at that institution, "and A looks after B in that institution".[252]

The Commission's view was that the broad definition of an educational abuse of trust:

> "... could lead to some highly questionable results ... [i]t would have the effect of creating a relationship of trust, for example, between a lecturer in a law school in one campus of a university and a student of medicine based in another campus even though there was no professional contact between the two".[253]

If that is questionable, the position now is even more so: if the two parties hypothesised by the Commission engage in sexual activity in Scotland, they commit an offence in England even though their conduct is lawful in this jurisdiction and even if they have never in their lives been south of the Border.

Abuse of trust of a mentally disordered person

Under s.46 of the 2009 Act,[254] the offence of sexual abuse of trust of a mentally disordered person is committed where A intentionally engages in a sexual activity with or directed towards a mentally disordered person, B,[255] and A is a person mentioned in s.46(2), which is in the following terms[256]: **2.55**

> "(a) a person providing care services to B,
> (b) a person who—
> (i) is an individual employed in, or contracted to provide services in or to, or
> (ii) not being the Scottish Ministers, is a manager of,
> a hospital, independent health care service or state hospital in which B is being given medical treatment."

The offence is one of strict liability (subject to defences discussed below) as regards the existence of B's mental disorder and the existence of the relationship of trust. "Care services" is further defined so as to be limited to services provided by a "care service" as defined by statute[257]: that is, the fact that A cares for B in some way does not in itself bring their relationship within the terms of this section.

The offence carries a maximum penalty, on summary conviction, of 12 months' imprisonment and/or a fine not exceeding the statutory maximum and, on conviction on indictment, of imprisonment for a term not exceeding five years and/or a fine.[258] There are no offences specified as possible alternative verdicts.[259] The offence may be committed outwith the United Kingdom where A is a UK national or resident and B is under the age of 18.[260]

---

[252] 2009 Act s.43(5)(b). The Commission recommended that this requirement apply generally, so that if B were a school pupil A would only be in position of trust regarding B if A looked after B at the school. See *Report*, para.4.131. That recommendation was reflected in the Bill as introduced, but its provisions were amended at Stage 2 to remove this requirement in respect of schools.

[253] *Report*, para.4.132 and fn.140.

[254] This derives, with modifications as recommended by the Scottish Law Commission, from s.313 of the Mental Health (Care and Treatment) (Scotland) Act 2003.

[255] "Mental disorder" has the same meaning as in s.328 of the Mental Health (Care and Treatment) (Scotland) Act 2003. See 2009 Act ss.17(3), 60(1).

[256] 2009 Act s.46(2).

[257] See 2009 Act s.46(3), (4), referring to the provisions of the Regulation of Care (Scotland) Act 2001.

[258] 2009 Act Sch.2.

[259] 2009 Act Sch.3. These are: coercing a person into being present during a sexual activity (s.5); coercing a person into looking at a sexual image (s.6); communicating indecently (s.7(1)); causing a person to see or hear an indecent communication (s.7(2)); causing an older child to participate in a sexual activity (s.31); or assault at common law.

[260] 2009 Act s.55, Sch.4 Pt 2. On extraterritorial jurisdiction, see above, para.1.39.

Defences

2.56 Five defences to the offence are established by s.47. These are as follows:

1.   A reasonably believed that B did not have a mental disorder;
2.   A reasonably believed that A was not in a position of trust in relation to B;
3.   B was A's spouse or civil partner;
4.   Where A was a person specified in s.46(2)(a), that a sexual relationship existed between A and B immediately before A began to provide care services to B; and
5.   Where A was a person specified in s.46(2)(b), "that immediately before B was admitted to the hospital (or other establishment) referred to in that provision or (where B has been admitted to that establishment more than once) was last admitted to it, such a relationship existed.

As with the defences to the offence of sexual abuse of trust,[261] the use of "reasonably believed" in the statutory wording is perplexing. The real issue is likely to be A's ignorance of the relevant facts, not that A considered and formulated an erroneous belief as to their possible existence. The Scottish Law Commission recommended that the defence be formulated as, "did not know, on reasonable grounds",[262] but for some reason this was expressed as "reasonably believed" in both the Commission's draft Bill and the 2009 Act. Once again, if A was unaware of B's mental disorder or the relationship of trust at the relevant time, then he should have in principle a defence if his *ignorance*— rather than belief—was reasonable, but this does depart from the literal wording of the statute.

---

[261] See above, para.2.53.

[262] *Report*, paras 4.124, 4.125, and see the Mental Health (Care and Treatment) (Scotland) Act 2003 s.313(3)(a)(i) ("did not know, and could not reasonably have been expected to know, that the other person was mentally disordered").

CHAPTER 3

THE PROSTITUTION (PUBLIC PLACES) (SCOTLAND) ACT 2007

The Scottish Law Commission viewed issues related to prostitution and pornog- **3.01**
raphy as outside the remit of its review,[1] and the 2009 Act accordingly makes no
provision in those areas. However, prostitution has been the subject of other legislation since the third edition of *The Criminal Law of Scotland* was published,
and so the relevant provisions are discussed here for completeness.[2] The offences
relating to sexual services of children and child pornography which were created
by the Protection of Children and Prevention of Sexual Offences (Scotland) Act
2005 are outlined in the first supplement to the third edition.[3]

The Background to the 2007 Act

Prior to this Act, the criminal law relating to prostitution in Scotland was **3.02**
principally concerned with prostitutes themselves or with those who sought
to control or profit from prostitution.[4] Prostitution was not itself criminal—
something which the 2007 Act does not change—but public solicitation and
importuning by a prostitute was (and remains) an offence.[5]

The actions of the client seeking the services of a prostitute in public, while
potentially criminal, were subject to the criminal law with rather less certainty.
Arguably, a male client could be guilty of the statutory offence of persistently
soliciting or importuning for immoral purposes in a public place,[6] but the offence was not intended for this purpose, does not appear to have in practice
been used in this way,[7] and its practical import would in any event have been
limited by the requirement of "persistence". It had been established for some
time that "kerb-crawling" by male motorists could be prosecuted as a common
law breach of the peace.[8] However, it must be doubted whether the soliciting of
a prostitute in an area known to be used for such purposes, perhaps even with
the toleration of the authorities,[9] would necessarily meet the *Smith v Donnelly*[10]
standard of, "conduct severe enough to cause alarm to ordinary people and
threaten serious disturbance to the community".[11]

---

[1] *Report*, paras 1.13–1.15.
[2] At the time of writing, proposals to create an offence of possession of extreme pornography
were under consideration by the Scottish Parliament as part of the Criminal Justice and Licensing
(Scotland) Bill, which was introduced into the Parliament in March 2009.
[3] Michael G.A. Christie, *The Criminal Law of Scotland: Third Edition Supplement* (Edinburgh:
SULI/ W. Green, 2005), para.31.15.
[4] See Gordon, *Criminal Law*, paras 36.39–36.47.
[5] Civic Government (Scotland) Act 1982 s.46. See also Criminal Law (Consolidation)
(Scotland) Act 1995 s.11(1)(b). The provisions are reviewed in Gordon, *Criminal Law*, para.36.40.
[6] Criminal Law (Consolidation) (Scotland) Act 1995 s.11(1)(b).
[7] Gane, *Sexual Offences*, 1992, pp.157, 158. In addition to the authorities cited there, see also
R. v Goddard (Nigel) (1991) 92 Cr. App. R. 185.
[8] Michael G.A. Christie, *Breach of the Peace* (Sevenoaks: Butterworths, 1990), paras 3.29,
3.30. See also J.S.F., "Breach of the Peace" (1962) 78 Scot. L. Rev. 73, 75.
[9] See Nicki Georghiou and Frazer McCallum, *Prostitution Tolerance Zones (Scotland) Bill*
(Scottish Parliament, 2002), SPICe Briefing 02/138, pp.9–12.
[10] *Smith (Pamela) v Donnelly*, 2002 J.C. 65. See Gordon, *Criminal Law*, para.41.05.
[11] *Smith v Donnelly*, 2002 J.C. 65, per Lord Coulsfield at [17]. See also Expert Group on
Prostitution in Scotland, *Being Outside: Constructing a Response to Street Prostitution* (Scottish
Executive, 2004), paras 11.14–11.16.

THE PROVISIONS OF THE 2007 ACT

3.03 The 2007 Act is based on the premise that the prior law was wrongly, "focused on those (predominately women) who sell sex on the street and not on those (predominately men) who purchase", and that there was, "a need to redress this balance".[12] Accordingly, the Bill which was introduced sought to replace the offence of soliciting and importuning by prostitutes under s.46 of the Civic Government (Scotland) Act 1982 with a single offence which would be applicable both to "buyers" and "sellers". That approach did not find favour as the Bill progressed through the Scottish Parliament.[13] The end result is that the offence under s.46 of the 1982 Act remains unchanged and s.1 of the 2007 Act creates two offences applicable only to "buyers". Its provisions are in the following terms:

> "(1) A person ('A') who, for the purpose of obtaining the services of a person engaged in prostitution, solicits in a relevant place commits an offence.
>
> (2) For the purposes of subsection (1) it is immaterial whether or not—
> (a)   A is in or on public transport,
> (b)   A is in a motor vehicle which is not public transport,
> (c)   a person solicited by A for the purpose mentioned in that subsection is a person engaged in prostitution.
>
> (3) A person ('B') who loiters in a relevant place so that in all the circumstances it may reasonably be inferred that B was doing so for the purpose of obtaining the services of a person engaged in prostitution commits an offence.
>
> (4) For the purposes of subsection (3) it is immaterial whether or not—
> (a)   B is in or on public transport,
> (b)   B is in a motor vehicle which is not public transport."

A "relevant place" is either a "public place" within the meaning of other legislation[14] or, "a place to which at the material time the public are permitted to have access (whether on payment or otherwise)".[15] Some guidance as to how it may "reasonably be inferred" that B was loitering for the purposes of prostitution may be found in the case law concerning the similarly constructed s.57 of the Civic Government (Scotland) Act 1982.[16] Factors such as the time of day, the accused's behaviour at the time or even at other places around that time will clearly be of importance.[17] A person committing either the two offences created by s.1 of the 2007 Act is liable on summary conviction to a fine not exceeding level 3 on the standard scale.[18]

---

[12]   Scottish Parliament, *Prostitution (Public Places) (Scotland) Bill: Policy Memorandum* (Scottish Parliament, 2006), para.2.

[13]   See Local Government and Transport Committee, *Stage 1 Report on the Prostitution (Public Places) (Scotland) Bill, 1st Report* (Scottish Parliament, 2007), SP Paper 711 (Session 2).

[14]   Prostitution (Public Places) (Scotland) Act 2007 s.1(6) adopts the definition in s.133 of the Civic Government (Scotland) Act 1982: "any place (whether a thoroughfare or not) to which the public have unrestricted access and includes (a) the doorways or entrances of premises abutting on any such place; and (b) any common passage, close, court, stair, garden or yard pertinent to any tenement or group of separately owned houses".

[15]   Prostitution (Public Places) (Scotland) Act 2007 s.1(6). For the purposes of the s.1(1) offence, it "includes a place which is visible from a place mentioned in paragraph (a) or (b)".

[16]   This makes it an offence to loiter without lawful authority in premises, "so that, in all the circumstances, it may reasonably be inferred that [the accused] intended to commit theft there".

[17]   See the case law discussed by Gordon *Criminal Law*, para.15.53, and also *Wilson v Barbour* [2009] HCJAC 30; 2009 S.L.T. 437, which emphasises the need for findings in fact to be made on all essentially relevant matters.

[18]   Prostitution (Public Places) (Scotland) Act 2007 s.1(5).

INDEX

My Best Book of

Early People

Margaret Hynes

KINGFISHER

Contents

KINGFISHER

Kingfisher Publications Plc,
New Penderel House,
283–288 High Holborn,
London WC1V 7HZ

www.kingfisherpub.com

Created for Kingfisher Publications Plc
by Picthall & Gunzi Limited

Author: Margaret Hynes
Designer: Dominic Zwemmer
Editor: Lauren Robertson
Consultant: Philip Wilkinson
Illustrators: Michael White, Peter Ross,
Marion Appleton, Angus McBride

First published by Kingfisher
Publications Plc 2003

10 9 8 7 6 5 4 3 2 1

1TR/0203/WKT/GLG(GLG)/128KMA

1TS/0804/WKT/GLG(GLG)/128MA/F

Copyright © Kingfisher
Publications Plc 2003

A CIP catalogue record for this book
is available from the British Library.

ISBN 0 7534 0821 X

Printed in China

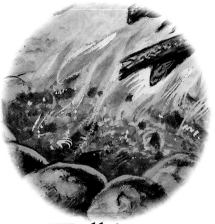

A human's hand can control a pencil.

Meet the humans

The first human-like creatures are known as 'hominids' and many scientists believe that they had the same ancestors as apes. The first hominid, called *Australopithecus*, lived in Africa between five and one million years ago. Over several million years, hominids learned to walk upright. Their brains also grew larger over time.

An ape's hand can only grasp objects.

Fingers and thumbs

Humans can pinch objects between their thumb and finger. This means that they can make things with their hands. Apes have short thumbs, so they can hold objects but cannot make things.

The march through time

The first apes lived 30 million years ago, and the first hominids lived about five million years ago. A long time ago, apes and hominids looked similar, but they evolved, or developed, separately.

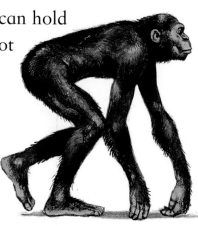

Proconsul
25 million years ago

Pliopithecus
15 million years ago

Australopithecus
from 5 million years ago

4

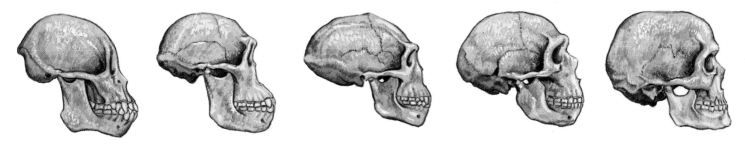

Proconsul   Australopithecus   Homo erectus   Neanderthal   Homo sapiens

Bigger heads for bigger brains

Archaeologists have found skulls which show that the brains
of hominids gradually got bigger over millions of years. As their
brains grew, hominids were able to do more difficult tasks. They
began to make tools, build shelters, use fire and hunt for food.

Homo habilis
from 2 million
years ago

Homo erectus
from 1.8 million
years ago

Neanderthal
from 100,000 to
35,000 years ago

Homo sapiens
from 1 million
years ago to today

5

The first toolmakers

 Two million years ago, a species of *Australopithecus* developed into a hominid, called *Homo*. *Homo* had a bigger brain and a more human-like face than *Australopithecus*. The earliest species of *Homo* could make stone tools and huts in which to live. This group was called *Homo habilis*, which means 'handy man'.

Handy man

As their brains grew in size, *Homo habilis* were able to do more difficult tasks. This species also had hands that could grip objects. So *Homo habilis* could make simple tools. They were able to build shelters from tree branches, leaves and stones like those in the camp below.

Large stones kept the branches of the shelter in place.

6

Finding food

Australopithecus lived in trees. They came down to the ground to find plants to eat or to gather berries (right). *Homo habilis* lived on the ground. They ate plants and meat. *Homo habilis* may also have taken the meat from dead animals abandoned by predators.

Australopithecus
gathering berries

Bones from scavenged
carcasses lay around
Homo habilis settlements.

Homo habilis used
stones to make
simple tools to cut
meat from carcasses.

Walking upright

A hominid called *Homo erectus*, or 'upright man', lived between 1.8 million and 200,000 years ago. *Homo erectus* gradually spread from Africa into China. They learned to use fire, so they were able to survive in Europe which was covered in ice at that time. *Homo erectus* had bigger brains than *Homo habilis*. They lived in caves and made many different tools.

Making fire
At first, *Homo erectus* used fires that were caused naturally by lightning. Later, they may have learned how to make fire by rubbing sticks together or striking stones to make a spark. They put stones around the fire to stop it spreading and to protect it from the wind.

A group of *Homo erectus* skins a dead animal.

Keeping warm
Homo erectus family groups gathered together around fires to keep warm. They probably also made fires to cook meat and to frighten away wild animals. Sometimes hunters also used fire to drive animals into traps.

A *Homo erectus*
family group
keeps warm
around a fire.

Storing berries

9

The Neanderthals

From 100,000 years ago, a type of *Homo sapiens* called Neanderthals lived in Europe, Asia and Africa. They had stocky bodies and brains as large as humans have today. During their lifetime, Europe and Asia were covered with ice. Neanderthals learned how to survive in the cold by making clothes from animal hides, or skins, by living in caves and by using fire.

Chopper   Scraper   Borer

Early toolkit

The Neanderthals made different tools for scraping, cutting and making holes in hides. These early toolmakers needed patience and practice to make stone and flint tools.

Animal horns were placed on top of the grave.

Neanderthal burials

The Neanderthals may have been the first hominids to care for their sick and bury their dead. They placed flowers around the dead body, and marked the grave with animal horns.

Neanderthals placed flowers in a grave.

The first tools

 *Homo habilis* made simple tools by knocking small pieces off stones to make sharp edges. Later, people made more complicated tools from a stone called flint. They made the tools by removing flakes from a piece of flint until it had a pointed edge. This is how hand axes were made. People also used the small flakes to make sharper tools, like knives and scrapers.

Hammerstone

Core

Making a hand axe

1 First the toolmaker chose a piece of flint, called the core. A hammerstone was used to knock large pieces off the flint.

Hammerstone

Antler hammer

Core

Flake

Special tools

The simplest tool used to make flint shapes was a hammerstone. It could break off large, thick flakes of flint. An antler hammer was used to remove small, thin flakes.

12

Flakes of flint

2 Then the hammerstone was used to take slightly smaller flakes of flint from the core until it became a rough oval shape.

Antler hammer

Small flakes

3 Finally, the hand axe was sharpened and given its finished shape. To do this, small flakes were chipped away from the core with the rounded end of an antler hammer.

Spearhead

Side scraper

End scraper

Hand axe

Knife

Quartz hand axe

Making do

When people could not find any flint, they made tools with quartz and other materials that they could shape easily.

13

Our early ancestors

Archaeologists believe that *Homo sapiens* first lived in Africa, then spread across the world. This group was called *Homo sapiens*, or 'wise man', because they had larger brains than earlier species and they learned to live in different climates. *Homo sapiens* are our early ancestors and they first lived about one million years ago.

Living well

Early *Homo sapiens* hunted animals such as mammoths and used the meat, skin and bones. They built homes from tree branches and animal skins to shelter from the cold. They also fished for food and made tools from wood, flint and bones.

This group of *Homo sapiens* hunters lived in southern Russia.

On the move

By 100,000 years ago, *Homo sapiens* lived in southern and eastern Africa. From there, they travelled hundreds of kilometres to the Middle East. By 11,000 years ago, *Homo sapiens* had reached the Americas.

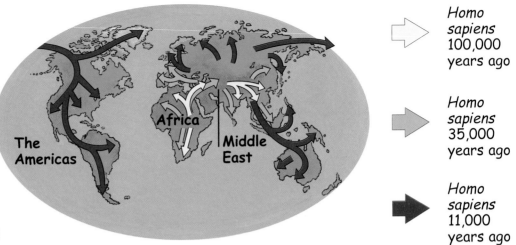

The Americas

Africa

Middle East

Homo sapiens 100,000 years ago

Homo sapiens 35,000 years ago

Homo sapiens 11,000 years ago

Homo sapiens built shelters of branches and animal skin.

The women scraped the animal skins clean.

Working together

During the last Ice Age, our ancestors worked in groups to hunt and capture large animals, such as woolly mammoths. They dug pits to trap an animal, and once it was caught, they killed it with sharp spears.

Hunters trap a woolly mammoth.

Mammoths were forced into pits by the hunters.

Life in the last Ice Age

Between 32,000 and 10,000 years ago, parts of the earth's surface were covered with ice. Cold periods like this are known as Ice Ages. Life was difficult for early humans during this Ice Age. Some food plants could not grow, and there was very little wood to make shelters. People had to find new foods, such as fish, and new building materials, such as animal bones.

New types of food

Early hunters learned how to track animals that lived in herds, such as reindeer. They used harpoons for killing seals and catching fish in the icy rivers.

Bone sewing needle

Antler harpoon head

Axe made of stone and antlers

Bone and antler tools

People used more bone and reindeer antlers than their ancestors. They made sewing needles from carved bone and used antlers to make handles for stone axes.

Early artists

The earliest pictures were painted 30,000 years ago, during the last Ice Age.

The first artists painted these pictures on rocks and the walls and roofs of caves. People also made sculptures using bone and clay. This early art can be found in many parts of the world. It tells us a lot about how our ancestors lived at that time, and about the animals that they hunted.

Australian art

Early artists in Australia painted colourful pictures of animals, rivers and rocks. They believed their ancestors became these things when they died.

Natural colours

Early artists made coloured paints from minerals in the soil and in rocks. Chalk was used to make white, charcoal made black and iron oxide made red. Brushes or pads of animal hair were used to apply paint to the rocks.

Iron oxide

Chalk

Charcoal

Stone lamp

Seeing in the dark

Artists often worked deep inside caves where there was no light. They burned animal fat in stone lamps so they could see what they were doing.

Animal fat in stone dish

The artist
holds a stone
lamp to light up
the cave wall.

European rock art

The most famous rock paintings
are in caves in Lascaux in France
(shown here) and Altimira in
Spain. Some show hunting
scenes and others show herds
of animals such as cattle, horses
and reindeer. Archaeologists
think these colourful pictures
may be 17,000 years old.

A time of plenty

About 10,000 years ago, the last Ice Age ended. Over time, forests grew and replaced the melting ice. New types of plants and animals evolved and lived in the forests, so our ancestors did not have to travel as far to find food. This gave people more time to make better tools. They ate well and lived longer, and so the world's population grew.

Settling down

People began to stay in one place for longer periods of time, so they built their homes to last. Hunters in Siberia (below) made shelters from animal bones and tusks, which they covered with animal skins, or hides.

The hunters cooked animals over an open fire.

Making bread

As the ice thawed in Africa and Asia, some areas became covered in grasses. People gathered the grasses, then separated the seeds from the stalks. They ground the seeds into flour and mixed it with water. The mixture was baked to make flat cakes of bread.

The women made bread from the flour.

In Siberia, shelters were made from animal hide, bones and tusks.

21

The first farmers

Groups of hunters around the world gradually learned how to farm. At first, they may have collected wild crops such as wheat. They also began to round up herds of the wild animals that they hunted. By 11,000 years ago, the first farmers were planting and growing their own crops in the Middle East. People also began to keep and breed different kinds of animals for milk and meat.

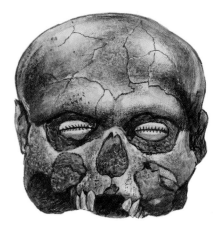

New styles of art

Farming was hard work, but people still found time to develop new styles of art. This human skull would have been covered in plaster and used in ceremonies.

This farming settlement in Turkey grew crops and herded animals.

Early farmers usually shared their houses with their animals.

An animal called a wild aurochs was the early ancestor of cattle.

22

Breeding crops and animals

Early farmers knew how to grow, or farm, the best crops. They took seeds from the biggest plants in a crop and sowed them to grow larger plants the next year. They also chose the healthiest animals for breeding.

Early farming towns

Farmers became rich, and they built more houses that were larger and grouped together. These groups of houses eventually grew into the first villages, towns and cities.

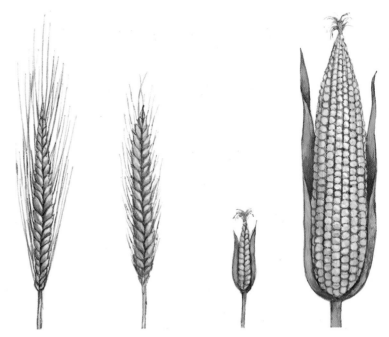

Wild wheat   Farmed wheat   Wild corn   Farmed corn

23

The Bronze Age

 **From about 5,500 years ago, people in western Asia started to use a metal called bronze to make tools and weapons.** This period is called the 'Bronze Age'. Bronze was formed by melting copper and tin together. It was harder and longer-lasting than other metals. Metalworking was a full-time job, so farmers had to grow enough food to feed all the metalworkers, too.

Casting bronze

Early metalworkers made bronze objects by a method called 'casting'. First, bronze bars were melted. Then the hot metal was poured into a mould and allowed to cool and set. Bronze could be cast into different shapes. Casting was done in a special area, away from the houses.

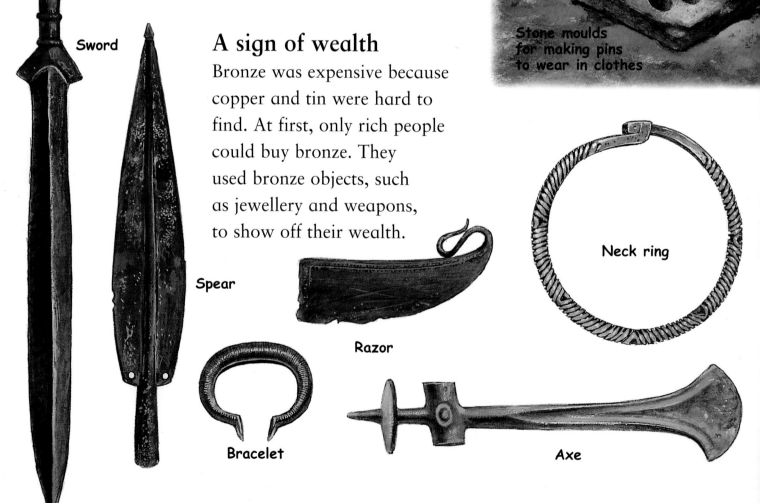

Stone moulds for making pins to wear in clothes

A sign of wealth

Bronze was expensive because copper and tin were hard to find. At first, only rich people could buy bronze. They used bronze objects, such as jewellery and weapons, to show off their wealth.

Sword

Spear

Razor

Neck ring

Bracelet

Axe

24

This man is preparing copper and tin for melting.

It needed two men to pour the heavy melted bronze into the mould.

Pins

Chariot decoration

Tweezers

Village life

More and more people wanted bronze objects, so groups of metalworkers started to sell the things that they made. They set up trading centres that grew into small villages. These settlements were often built close to rivers, where the rich soil was also good for farming.

25

Life in the Iron Age

The metal that we call iron was discovered in the Middle East about 3,300 years ago. People began to make weapons and other objects out of iron, and ironworking soon spread to Europe. Some groups of people, such as the Celts, used iron weapons to fight other peoples and take over their lands. The Celts become very powerful in this way. They built hill forts that were large enough for people, houses and herds of animals.

An Iron Age
fort in Europe

Building walls

The Celts protected their forts by surrounding them with deep ditches. The earth from the ditches was used to make high barriers that gave extra protection. Iron weapons were then used to fight off any attackers.

Massive gate
to protect the
fort's entrance

A useful metal

At first, only important people such as chiefs had iron weapons. Later, everyone used tools made of iron. Iron is easy to sharpen, and can be strengthened by banging it with a hammer, so it is a useful weapon.

Iron dagger

Iron swords have been found that are more than 2,000 years old.

Houses built inside the fort

Land set aside for herds of animals

Wooden fence surrounding the fort to protect from attackers

Barrier made out of earth from a ditch

27

Civilization begins

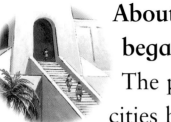

About 8,000 years ago, towns began to grow into cities.
The people who lived in these cities built temples and palaces, and began to write things down. In these communities, there were many different jobs for people to do. This new way of life in the city is what we now call civilization. Civilization began in an area of the Middle East called Mesopotamia.

Cuneiform

The people of Mesopotamia wrote by making marks in clay tablets with a wedge-shaped reed. This writing is called 'cuneiform', which means 'wedge' in Greek.

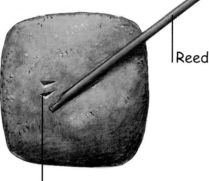

Reed

Wedge-shaped mark on clay

First letters

Writing was invented in Mesopotamia about 5,200 years ago. At first, people wrote lists of the things that they traded. Soon, they started to write down stories.

The people of Mesopotamia

Mesopotamians became wealthy through farming and trading. In the city of Ur, rich people filled their houses with painted pottery, sculptures and pretty jewellery.

This type of early temple is called a ziggurat.

Making a piece of pottery

Grinding flour for bread

29

How we know

There are no written records that tell us about the earliest peoples.
Archaeologists have to study bones, pots and anything else left behind by our early ancestors to find out about their everyday lives. First, archaeologists dig in the ground to look for clues. Then they study what they have found, sometimes using special scientific equipment.

Using science

A scientific method known as 'radiocarbon dating' helps archaeologists to find out an object's age. X-rays are used to examine mummies without damaging them.

Ice man

In 1991, the 5,300-year-old body of a man was found high in the Alps in Europe. It had been preserved by ice. Scientists who studied the body learnt that the man may have been murdered.

Layers of history

The deeper an object is buried, the older it is likely to be. Archaeologists dig carefully to avoid causing any damage. Sometimes they find layers of objects in the order that they were used in history.

Archaeologist mapping the site

Archaeologist brushing away soil

Ancient Chinese statues of warriors

Glossary

ancestor A dead relative from a long time ago in history.

ape A hairy mammal that has two arms and two legs and a short tail. Apes can walk upright or on all fours.

archaeologist A person who digs up objects left behind by earlier people, and studies them to find out how our ancestors lived.

Australopithecus Ape-like animals that lived between five and one million years ago and showed the first human characteristics.

Bronze Age A period in the history of humans when tools, weapons and jewellery were made out of the metal bronze.

casting A way of making shaped objects, such as weapons, by pouring hot metal into a mould.

crop A plant that is grown by people as food for themselves or their animals.

fertile Land that produces good crops is described as fertile.

fort A settlement or building that is protected by walls and trenches.

Homo erectus The scientific name for our ancestors who lived from 1.8 million years ago and were the first to walk upright.

Homo habilis The scientific name for our ancestors who lived from two million years ago and were the first to make simple tools.

Homo sapiens The scientific name for our most recent ancestors. *Homo sapiens* lived from one million years ago until the present day, and have developed into modern-day humans.

Ice Age A period of time when much of the earth's surface is covered with ice. There have been a number of Ice Ages over the past two million years. The last Ice Age ended 10,000 years ago. The warmer periods of time between Ice Ages are known as interglacials.

Iron Age A period in the history of humans when tools, weapons and jewellery were made out of the metal iron.

mammoth A type of hairy elephant that lived in the most recent Ice Age, but that is now extinct.

Neanderthal Human-like creatures that lived from 100,000 to 35,000 years ago. They walked upright and made tools.

predators Animals that hunt and prey on other animals are known as predators. Sabre-toothed tigers are predators.

species Groups of plants or animals that have similar characteristics.

temple A large building where people gather to pray to a god or gods.

tool An object that is used to carry out tasks. For example, our ancestors used hammering tools to make axes from stones.

Index